Know Your New Zealand ...

Birds

Lynnette Moon

Photographs by
Geoff Moon

NEW
HOLLAND

Acknowledgements

I am grateful to Belinda Cooke and New Holland Publishers (NZ) for the opportunity to write this book and especially thank Matt Turner for his interest and encouragement. I could not have completed the work without the guidance and enthusiastic support of my husband, Geoff Moon. His wealth of knowledge never ceases to amaze and inspire me. This book has been a joy to write.

Lynnette Moon

First published in 2006 by New Holland Publishers (NZ) Ltd
Auckland • Sydney • London • Cape Town

www.newhollandpublishers.co.nz

218 Lake Road, Northcote, Auckland, New Zealand
Unit 1, 66 Gibbes Street, Chatswood, NSW 2067, Australia
86-88 Edgware Road, London W2 2EA, United Kingdom
80 McKenzie Street, Cape Town 8001, South Africa

Copyright © 2006 in text: Lynnette Moon
Copyright © 2006 in photography: Geoff Moon
Copyright © 2006 in illustration: Page 8, New Holland Publishers (UK) Ltd
Copyright © 2006 New Holland Publishers (NZ) Ltd

ISBN: 978 1 86966 089 5

Managing editor: Matt Turner
Editor: Brian O'Flaherty/Punaromia
Design: Julie McDermid/Punaromia
Cover design: Nick Turzynski, redinc

A catalogue record for this book is available from the National Library of New Zealand

10 9 8 7 6 5 4 3 2

Front cover photographs clockwise from left: New Zealand kingfisher, New Zealand falcon, pied stilt, New Zealand pigeon. Back cover photographs, from top: northern royal albatross, kaka, tomtit, North Island kokako.

Colour reproduction by Pica Digital Pte Ltd, Singapore
Printed by Tien Wah Press (Pte) Ltd

Contents

Introduction

The birds around us

This book aims to help readers with an interest in birds to feel confident in identifying them. It can be challenging to recognise the appearance of certain birds. Also, we soon realise that identification sometimes relies on our familiarity with a particular flight pattern or call, when the bird itself cannot be clearly seen.

Unique birds

New Zealand is home to many unique birds, seen only in this country. Two examples are the kakapo and the kiwi, both flightless and nocturnal in habit. The kakapo is also the largest, heaviest parrot in the world, and the kiwi is unique in being the only bird in the world with its nostrils situated at the tip of a long, sensitive bill. A number of other birds are either flightless or very weak fliers.

The islands of New Zealand separated from the large supercontinent of Gondwanaland more than 70 million years ago. Because of the country's isolation and lack of mammalian predators (at that time), birds evolved unique characteristics. As they did not need to fly to escape ground-dwelling predators, some birds developed features such as large size and loss of flight. Many evolved with a dull plumage that seemed to blend with their habitats. This camouflage was probably protection from a few avian predators, for example the raptors. Among these was the New Zealand eagle, the largest bird of prey ever known. The New Zealand eagle later became extinct as its main food supply, the moa, was eliminated through hunting by Maori.

As well as large, flightless birds, New Zealand has always been home to a variety of flighted birds. One of these was the distinctive huia, now extinct. The bills of the male and female huia differed more than any other bird in the world, with the female's remarkable bill being very much longer and more curved than the male's.

Habitats

New Zealand is geographically diverse and within a comparatively small landmass the variety of habitats provides a home for many species of birds.

These environments include the sea, coastline and offshore islands, open countryside, wetlands, forests and high country. Birds also live within urban areas.

Some birds occupy several habitats. One of the most notable of these is the kingfisher, finding food in the forest, open pastureland, wetlands and (particularly in winter) along the coast. Other birds, especially migrants, move through one habitat to another, according to their seasonal needs, and in search of particular food. Some birds migrate within New Zealand, while many coastal waders migrate to and from eastern Siberia and Alaska in autumn and spring.

The seas surrounding New Zealand are rich in marine life, attracting a variety of seabirds. These include two-thirds of the world's species of tubenosed birds, such as albatrosses. New Zealand, particularly its numerous offshore islands, plays an essential part in providing shelter for nesting sites for birds that spend long periods fishing at sea.

European settlers established some of the passerine (perching) birds, as nostalgic reminders of their homeland. These birds are more commonly seen in open country and urban regions. Other birds, such as pheasants, were introduced to be used as game birds.

Some birds that are now a familiar sight throughout New Zealand were self-introduced, particularly from Australia.

Over a period of time certain bird species have diminished or become extinct as a result of predation and loss of habitat through large-scale clearing of forest and wetlands for agricultural use. Other birds have survived because they have been able to adapt to different environments and diets. Still others exist with the aid of a protected environment.

Breeding

An interesting aspect of bird behaviour is the varying patterns in breeding. Some species, for example ducks and pheasants, lay large clutches of 10 or more eggs. This is necessary as the chicks or ducklings, being precocial (able to run after hatching), suffer a high mortality rate due to the hazards of predation and accidents that occur near their vulnerable nest sites.

Other species, such as petrels and shearwaters, lay only one egg per clutch. Their nests on offshore islands are not so easily predated and are therefore more likely to be successful.

The egg clutch size in small passerine birds like finches varies with the availability of food. When food is plentiful, they are likely to nest several times in one season.

If the first nest is lost through storms or by predation, birds will often re-nest.

In ancient New Zealand, however, birds did not face this uncertainty of survival. As there was no need to be wary of predators, many lived long lives and reproduced slowly.

Predators

With the arrival of humans in New Zealand, mammalian predators were introduced. Vegetation was burned to clear land, destroying vast areas of birds' habitats. Birds were a major source of food for Maori. They used dogs to hunt large flightless birds, speared plump forest birds like the New Zealand pigeon and also harvested seabirds in large numbers. The Polynesian rat, kiore, was a proficient climber, taking the eggs and chicks of birds nesting in trees. Maori used feathers in cloaks, particularly from kiwi, pigeon and kaka, with the prized huia feathers as special ornamentation.

The agile black ship rat that escaped from the boats of explorers and sealers proved to be an even more destructive predator than the kiore.

With the later arrival of European settlers, other browsing animals were introduced. Pigs and goats caused damage to foliage in forest habitats. Dogs and feral cats proved to be devastating predators. The new settlers also brought guns for hunting. Flightless birds were easy prey for rats, cats and dogs. The later introduction of the brush-tailed possum and stoats has proved disastrous. Being active climbers, possums have also predated the nests of tree-dwelling forest birds, taking both eggs and chicks. Possums have foraged relentlessly on foliage throughout tracts of luxuriant forest trees, causing widespread destruction in many regions of native forest habitat.

The mammalian predators continue to be a threat to birdlife, except in certain well-controlled areas. Animals introduced for the purpose of game shooting, such as deer, have caused widespread damage to vegetation, affecting the food supply of some species.

Sanctuaries

Conservation programmes have contributed greatly to the preservation of endangered species and their habitats. Numerous islands lie off the coast of New Zealand and as some are predator-free, they provide sanctuary for many endangered native birds.

One island, Tiritiri Matangi, is within easy reach of Auckland and readily accessible to visitors. The larger Kapiti Island near Wellington is home to many rare and endangered species. Permits are easily obtained to visit.

In recent years the Department of Conservation has selected certain mainland areas of native forest as special 'islands', where intensive control of predators has resulted in an increase in the breeding success of many native bird species as well as the flourishing regrowth of original vegetation. Some native bird species that had previously disappeared from these regions have been re-introduced from offshore sanctuaries.

These mainland 'island' sanctuaries include the King Country Mapara Forest, the native forest and reservoir area of Karori in Wellington, and the 'Ark in the Park' established in the Waitakere Ranges of Auckland.

How to use this guide

Birds are listed in this guidebook in taxonomic order. Taxonomy is the scientific method of classifying living and extinct organisms, according to their particular anatomy. So in this book we begin with the kiwi and finish with the magpie.

Closely related species are grouped together as a genus (plural: genera). Related genera are grouped as a family. Related families in turn are grouped into an order. The first part of a bird's scientific name is the genus. The second name refers to the species and the third name, where applicable, gives the sub-species. For example, the sooty shearwater or muttonbird (page 16) is named *Puffinus griseus*. The genus *Puffinus* belongs to the family Procellariidae, which contains the shearwaters, diving petrels, fulmars, prions and gadfly petrels. In turn, this family belongs to the order Procellariiformes, the tubenosed birds.

Under each entry in the book the approximate size of the bird is given in centimetres, and this is the length measured from the tip of the bill to the tip of the tail. In some instances, when applied to long-legged birds such as stilts or herons, the length is measured to the feet when the bird is in flight with the legs extended beyond its tail.

We describe birds as being endemic, native or introduced. Endemic means that a bird has evolved and occurs and breeds naturally only in New Zealand. Birds like kiwi and kaka are correctly known as endemic. Native refers to birds that have arrived in New Zealand by themselves (self-introduced) and become established here, like the Australian coot and spur-winged plover, but these birds are also found in other countries. Introduced birds, such as blackbirds and finches, are birds brought to New Zealand by humans.

Other information given in the side panels includes, where applicable, key Maori names, abundance, distribution and threat status. The main text entry for each species includes a general description of appearance, features and characteristics, habitat, and nesting activities.

Note that there are seasonal and sexual differences in certain birds. Examples of these are the starling, which displays a bright star-like seasonal plumage in late summer, and also the male and female paradise shelduck, which always display obvious sexual differences in their plumage colour.

Fortunately, most of the varied habitats within New Zealand are readily accessible to us, and the birds covered in this guide are those we are most likely to observe, or are relatively well known.

However enthusiastic we may be in learning more about birds' activities, it is important to take particular care when they are nesting. If nests are too closely approached, or foliage removed, birds are likely to desert their nests. As well, this may allow a predator easy access.

For more detailed information on all the birds of New Zealand, please refer to other guidebooks listed in the bibliography on page 174.

Bird topography

These are the terms commonly used by ornithologists to describe parts of birds.

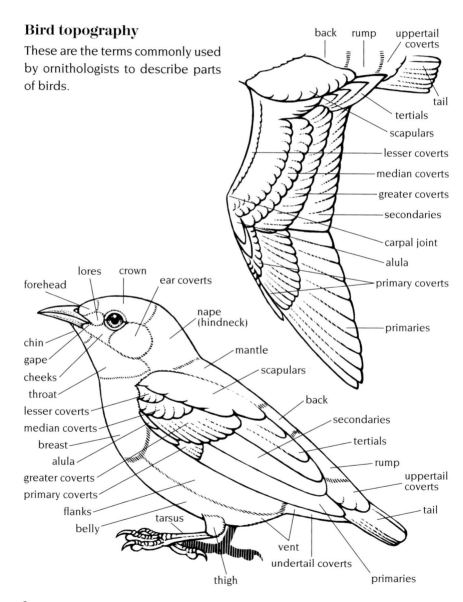

Glossary

Aquatic: frequenting water.
Australasia: Australia, New Guinea, the south-western Pacific and New Zealand.
Catch on wing/To hawk: catching prey in the air, or in flight.
Ceres: small fleshy covering of upper bills in certain birds, e.g. pigeons.
Cosmopolitan: frequenting many countries.
Coverts: feathers that cover the bases of main wing feathers and tail feathers.
Crustacean: invertebrate enclosed in hard outer shell, e.g. shrimp.
Cryptic: a colouring that serves to conceal or camouflage.
Endangered: likely to become extinct if not managed carefully.
Endemic: found only in a certain country and nowhere else, e.g. kiwi.
Fledged: fully feathered and able to fly.
Flight feathers: the long, well-developed feathers of the wing.
Honeyeater: feeding on nectar/honeydew.
Honeydew: a sugary substance exuded by aphids and invertebrates.
Introduced: a bird brought to New Zealand by humans, not by its own efforts.
Invertebrate: animal without a spinal column, e.g. insect, worm.
Juvenile: a young bird in its first feathered plumage.
Krill: type of shrimp. Common in southern waters.
Migrant: a bird that regularly moves to another area away from its breeding site.
Mollusc: an invertebrate with a soft body and often a hard outer shell, e.g. snail.
Native: birds naturally found in a country or self-introduced, e.g. silvereye.
Nocturnal: active at night.
Omnivorous: feeding on a variety of animal and plant food.
Passerine: order of perching birds.
Plankton: small, dense floating animal life and plant life in the sea.
Precocial: active soon after birth.
Predator: animal that takes birds or their eggs or chicks.
Race: a population of a species occurring in a different geographical region.
Sedentary: non-migratory. Seldom moves far from its birthplace.
Social/Sociable: choose to live in the company of its own kind and similar.
Speculum: iridescent patch on the secondary feathers of ducks.
Subspecies: a geographical race that has differences from the species.
Territorial: a state in which a species attempts to evict others from an area.
Threatened: species that are low in numbers or declining in number.
Wattles: coloured fleshy tissue on either side of the gape (edge of beak where it opens), e.g. kokako.

Brown kiwi

■ Widespread throughout New Zealand.

■ Not common.

■ Threatened species, protected by law.

Length:
40–45 cm

Scientific Name:
Apteryx australis

Maori Names:
Kiwi, tokoeka, rowi

Status:
Endemic

Of all New Zealand birds, kiwi are the most well known, yet these secluded, nocturnal birds are seldom seen in the wild. Kiwi are related to moa and are the smallest of the ancient, flightless ratite family, with brown kiwi being the most common of the three main species of kiwi. They inhabit the forests of Northland, Westland and Stewart Island. During the day the birds roost in burrows or the hollows of fallen logs and venture out at night to feed, occasionally calling in prolonged, shrill whistles. An exception to this feeding behaviour is the Stewart Island brown kiwi, sometimes seen on dull days or at dusk, feeding on sand hoppers hidden among kelp on the beach.

Kiwi possess a number of unique features. They retain only vestiges of wings within their thick coats of glistening hair-like feathers, have no tails, and are the only birds in the world with nostrils situated at the tips of their bills. Kiwi are poorly sighted, but gifted with acute senses of smell and hearing, so feed by scenting and listening for insects, snuffling as they shuffle along the ground and probe in the earth with their bills. The birds smell fallen, ripe fruit and detect movements of invertebrates in the leaf litter, and by feeling vibrations can locate earthworms and grubs several centimetres below the surface of the soil.

Fine sensory whiskers at the base of their bills guide them in detecting obstacles, and their strong feet are useful in digging out insects as well as for running swiftly and exerting forceful kicks when attacked.

Breeding may be dependent on an abundance of food and ideal conditions, so kiwi are erratic in their nesting behaviour, although most nesting occurs in early summer. Nest sites are likely to be located in burrows or hollows of fallen trees, where the birds lay one or two very large eggs.

The kiwi population has decreased due to predation by stoats, feral cats and dogs, and habitat destruction, so some have been placed in protective bird sanctuaries or zoos. These are the places where kiwi are most likely to be seen.

Because of the predation of chicks, a recovery programme has been established that entails removal and incubation of eggs. When hatched these kiwi chicks are reared for several months before being released into the wild when they are strong enough to attempt to protect themselves from predators.

New Zealand dabchick

■ Inhabit clear lakes and lagoons of North Island west coast, Rotorua and Taupo.

■ Locally common.

■ Threatened species; protected.

Length: 28 cm

Scientific Name: *Poliocephalus rufopectus*

Maori Name: Weweia

Status: Endemic

New Zealand dabchicks are now found only in the North Island and are located on the sand-dune lakes and lagoons of the North Island west coast and the lakes at Rotorua and Taupo. Birds are often seen near the boat ramp opposite the Rotorua municipal golf course and the old wharf near Tokaanu. In Auckland a few birds occupy the lake at Western Springs. They prefer clear water and the safety of sheltered lakes, with banks fringed by protective rushes.

Dabchicks belong to the grebe family. These dumpy little birds with sharp beaks have a habit of fluffing out their rear-end feathers. As they swim swiftly, dabchicks bob their heads in an alert forward motion.

The birds are entirely aquatic, with lobe-webbed feet set well back on their bodies. Unlike ducks, dabchicks' flattened toes are each bordered with a web of skin, making it difficult for them to walk on land. Very efficient at swimming and diving, they feed while submerged on small fish, tadpoles, invertebrates and molluscs and can remain under water for 10 to 25 seconds. Frequently diving in search of food, the birds will suddenly disappear from sight, only to reappear 10 or more metres away, sometimes as far away as 50 metres.

Dabchicks are rarely seen in flight, although during courtship they sometimes skim across the surface of the water chasing after one another. It seems that they migrate from one lake to another at night.

Just as these birds spend their lives on the water they also build their nests on water. Nests are floating, small raft-like clumps of waterweed and rush stems anchored to reeds or trailing branches of willow. They are often tucked away in rushes or sometimes even built under the floors of lakeside boatsheds. If parents need to leave their nests, they first cover the two or three eggs with protective waterweed and as a result the eggs soon become brown-stained.

Like all grebes, dabchicks carry chicks on the back of one of the parents while the other dives for food. Chicks are fed mainly aquatic invertebrates, tadpoles and molluscs with occasional feathers as protection against possible sharp fish bones. The family remains together until the chicks are fully grown.

During winter months flocks of dabchicks often congregate on larger lakes, such as Lake Wairarapa.

Northern royal albatross

Albatrosses are the largest of all flying birds. Majestic royal albatrosses spend most of their lives flying thousands of kilometres across southern oceans, effortlessly gliding through turbulent wind currents and surviving in the severest gales. The long, narrow forearms of their wings are fixed rigid, enabling them to sustain a dynamic, soaring flight.

Across the depths of the oceans, birds are often seen following ships to catch scraps, although they also occur in inland waters, particularly during winter. But to observe albatrosses closely it is possible to visit a nesting colony at Taiaroa Head on the Otago Peninsula. This is the only inhabited mainland albatross colony in the world. Colonies are usually sited on windy slopes, assisting birds to take off and hover in air currents before landing.

In order to feed, albatrosses must alight on the water, making clumsy splashes as they catch fish near the surface of the sea. The favoured albatross food is squid and these are usually caught at night when squid rise near the surface of the sea. The birds are attracted to bait and squid caught on longlines used by commercial fishing vessels, with the result that many thousands of birds are drowned every year.

Albatrosses belong to the family of tubenosed birds that spend most of their lives at sea. The salt gland at the base of the tubenose on the bills ejects extra concentrated salt that is inadvertently consumed in their diet.

Birds return to their nesting colonies in October or November, with males usually arriving first, and as the pair meet they greet each other in elaborate displays of wing clapping and groans, with heads held skywards. Although they may revisit the colony when younger, birds do not breed until they are about nine years old and nest every second year. They live long lives, with one known to have lived for 60 years.

Nests consist of grasses combined with small sods of earth that are formed into mounds. Single eggs are laid, and chicks remain in their nests for about eight months where they are fed on regurgitated fish and squid by both parents.

As longline fishing kills thousands of birds each year, there are regulations to help protect them from this danger. However, many fishing vessels ignore the guidelines, operating illegally and often avoiding prosecution.

Sooty shearwater

■ Widespread on the southern islands.

■ Abundant.

■ Protected.

Length: 44 cm

Scientific Name:
Puffinus griseus

Maori Name:
Titi

Status:
Native

Sooty shearwaters are also known as muttonbirds and are most familiar in that a traditional Maori harvest of the fattest chicks is permitted on some islands in Foveaux Strait and around Stewart Island. Sooty shearwaters breed, fish and migrate together in vast flocks. They are one of the world's most common birds, and with a population exceeding 20 million, sooty shearwaters are New Zealand's most prolific breeding birds. Many varieties of seabirds successfully breed in New Zealand, as the surrounding southern seas are so rich in their marine-life diet.

After breeding in the far south, sooty shearwaters are most likely to be seen in late summer as they migrate northwards to feed in the North Pacific. Massive flocks of the birds, stretching for several kilometres, fly along east coast locations. They are thought to move in a clockwise direction around the Pacific Ocean.

Sooty shearwaters fly quickly, often swooping high and then gliding just a few centimetres above the sea's surface. Sometimes birds fly alone, but more commonly they form flocks, feeding together on small fish, krill and squid. They catch fish by plunging into the sea, then pursuing their prey several metres just beneath the surface. In calm weather when the sea is still, large rafts of the birds are often seen resting on the surface of the water.

Even though shearwaters spend months circling over many thousands of kilometres of the Pacific, they return to their former breeding grounds on the headlands of southern islands in September, coming ashore at night. The birds nest under boulders and bushes or in caves, but most choose the safety of chambers at the end of old burrows and these are cleaned out and lined with fresh leaves and twigs. On departure and return to colonies after fishing, shearwaters are noisy, calling out in loud, rasping moans as they crash to the ground with a thud, before entering their burrows.

Each pair lays a single egg in November and chicks are first fed on regurgitated fish paste followed later by small fish. Parents leave their well-fed chicks behind to begin their migration north, and the chicks follow later.

Sooty shearwaters may be affected by the development of land, the overharvesting of chicks as well as drift netting by commercial fishing fleets. Protection of some colonies ensures overall security of population.

White-faced storm petrel

These delicate storm petrels are the smallest of the tubenosed birds and the smallest of New Zealand's seabirds, being scarcely the size of a blackbird. They are the most common storm petrels seen around New Zealand coasts and the best time to see them is during the breeding season from August to March. Like albatrosses and shearwaters, storm petrels are tubenosed, with the tubenose joined on the top of their bills.

At sea the birds are easily recognised by their particular dancing movements as they flit over the surface of the sea. With their long, webbed toes and dangling feet they skip and prance on the water between short glides, constantly searching for plankton and small crustaceans. As the birds spend much of their time feeding close to the sea surface this results in a rather erratic flight and they are also known as Jesus Christ birds, because they appear to walk on water. At times, storm petrels may be seen just resting on the sea, either alone or in loose flocks.

Most of them migrate to the tropical waters of the eastern Pacific and the coasts of Ecuador and Peru after breeding. But they return to their nesting colonies on many of the small islands off the coasts of the North and South Islands to breed.

Storm petrels sometimes nest in rock crevices, but usually tiny burrows are excavated into fine soil. At the end of the burrows are the nests, where leaves are placed to cover the earth. With each nest set about 50 centimetres apart, these colonies form a fragile honeycomb of burrows that could easily collapse underfoot. Like all shearwaters and petrels, one egg is laid and the chick is fed on regurgitated fish paste by both parents.

Soon after dark, after fishing at sea, hundreds of the birds arrive all at once, circling and swirling above their nesting colony, before dropping gently and landing in the scrub, then scuttling to their burrows. With no disturbance or sound, the dainty, silver-white storm petrels seem to drift to the ground like the silent fall of snowflakes.

White-faced storm petrels are sometimes affected by the predation of rats and native weka, and in southern seas skuas (large, predatory seabirds) may attack the small birds. However, in colonies on predator-free offshore islands and small coastal islets the birds continue to thrive.

Yellow-eyed penguin

- Inhabit lower east coast of South Island.
- Uncommon.
- Threatened species; protected.

Length: 65 cm

Scientific Name: *Megadyptes antipodes*

Maori Name: Hoiho

Status: Endemic

Found only in New Zealand, yellow-eyed penguins are the world's rarest penguins, inhabiting locations along the lower east coast of the South Island, from Banks Peninsula to Campbell Island. They tend to remain near their coastal roosting and nesting sites all year, fishing at sea and coming ashore late in the day to roost. The birds are sharp-eyed and very wary, scanning for predators ashore.

Like all penguins, their sleek, tightly packed, narrowed feathers are waterproof and their flat wings have been adapted to flippers. Flippers are used to great advantage in rapidly propelling the birds as they pursue fish, squid and krill under water. With razor-sharp bills the birds grasp fish that are then swallowed whole. After a day of fishing, penguins swim ashore, shake off excess water and preen briefly, then these stocky, upright birds waddle from the sea, balanced by their flippers as they shuffle across the sand.

Yellow-eyed penguins are not sociable birds, roosting within scattered seaside foliage, quite separated and hidden from other penguin pairs. They nest where they roost all year, tucked among coastal scrub, flax, hollows of old forest trees and boulders. In these sites penguins are protected from sun and storms, but the birds often need to trudge up sand banks in the evening to reach their roosts where they then call to each other in piercing vibrant trills.

Flattened-out scrapes, lined with grasses, serve as nests where one or two eggs are laid. Chicks are fed on regurgitated fish and leave the nest when they are independent at about 15 weeks of age.

After breeding, adults feed intensively at sea before returning ashore and hiding away in seclusion as they moult all their feathers over a three-week period. The feathers fall off in tufts, allowing new plumage to develop, but as the birds do not eat during this time they become weak and may even starve.

Particularly when moulting and nesting, yellow-eyed penguins are vulnerable to predators that include stoats, feral cats and stray dogs. Nesting sites are affected by land development and the birds sometimes suffer from food shortages and disease.

Recovery and management programmes now help protect these rare penguins and their habitat. Observation platforms in certain locations along the east coast of the South Island allow easy viewing of the penguins' activities.

Blue penguin

Blue penguins are the smallest species of penguins in the world and are commonly seen around New Zealand coasts from North Cape to Stewart Island, including many offshore islands. They are also the only penguins to come ashore after dark to roost. Although called blue penguins, their compact feathers are generally blue-grey, sometimes appearing metallic grey. Like all penguins, their dark back colouring and white breasts are camouflage from predators both above and below the sea.

The birds spend all day at sea, usually swimming alone or in small groups. With wings adapted to flippers, blue penguins are very agile in the water, tending to fish inshore near roosting sites, like yellow-eyed penguins. Sometimes they just float, resting on their sides before suddenly diving rapidly. Although blue penguins have been seen at depths of 50 metres, they usually feed close to the surface on small fish and crustaceans.

At night they come ashore to roost, and although these penguins are very agile in the sea, they are clumsy on land, shuffling and stumbling over stones and rocks, balanced by their outstretched flippers. Not usually standing as upright as other penguins, they tend to lean forward as they scurry ashore to the rocky crevices, caves and burrows that serve as roosts for the night.

Roosting sites may also be used as nesting sites, and although blue penguins are known to move inland as far as 150 metres up steep slopes and along streambeds to nest beneath tree roots, more often nests are along the upper shore. These may be in caves, rock clefts, burrows and even under seaside baches. Before birds settle down for the night they are restless, squawking and wailing, especially when nesting, so for this reason sites chosen under baches are not popular with their human occupants.

Blue penguins usually lay two eggs and chicks leave the nest at eight weeks of age. Parents then spend time feeding themselves well and fattening up before their annual moult, when they remain hidden away and not eating for a period of two to three weeks. Fattening up is necessary, as it not only helps to prevent penguins from starving but also insulates them from the cold, as all their feathers fall out over this short period.

Blue penguins can be affected by food shortages and sometimes disease. They are also vulnerable to attack by stray dogs, cats and stoats.

Australasian gannet

The spectacular sight of Australasian gannets plunging head-first into the sea is familiar around New Zealand coasts. Sometimes these birds fish alone and at other times in flocks, especially when following shoals of fish. They are easily recognised by their wide wings edged with black, pointed black tails and yellow-gold capped heads.

When fishing, gannets frequently plummet like arrows, from as high as 30 metres, into deep water. They are often seen sweeping and gliding across the sea, only to suddenly drop vertically with heads and wings outstretched before entering the water at high speed with wings folded against their bodies. When fishing in loose flocks over shoals of fish, gannets make quick, low dives. They feed on small fish, anchovies and squid, seizing the fish in their strong, serrated bills and usually swallowing it while on the sea surface. Birds also fish in inner waters, sometimes skimming along a line of breakers where they may make shallow dives close to the beach. After fishing, birds often rest on the sea.

Gannets nest in dense colonies on small islands and jutting cliffs, with most in the North Island. Three mainland colonies have been formed: at Cape Kidnappers, Muriwai and Farewell Spit, and gannets congregate at these nesting sites in early spring, with males usually arriving first. In graceful courtship displays the pairs raise their heads and bills, squawking loudly as they shake their heads and touch bills.

Seaweed and grasses are cemented with dirt and excreta to form mounds for nests and in the colonies they are separated from one another by about a metre. They lay one egg and these are incubated under the gannets' carefully placed, black, webbed feet, with the birds then entirely covering them with their breast feathers.

After fledging, chicks leave the nests and cross the Tasman Sea, spending four to five years around the coast of Australia. They then return to the colonies where they were born, to begin their own breeding. Mature adult birds tend to be sedentary, fishing over the inshore sea not far out from the coast.

Controlled access to nesting colonies so that birds are not disturbed has led to an increase in numbers of gannets. Human interference can disrupt a colony and lead to predation of eggs by gulls, but behind protective fences birds can easily be observed at close range without disturbance.

Black shag

Cosmopolitan. Widespread on inland waterways and coasts.

Common.

Protected.

Length: 88 cm

Scientific Name:
Phalacrocorax carbo novaehollandiae

Maori Name:
Kawau

Status:
Native

In New Zealand, cormorants are referred to as shags and 14 species of these birds exist throughout the country. Black shags are a cosmopolitan species, commonly seen on both inland lakes and rivers as well as along sheltered harbours and coasts. They are the largest shags seen in New Zealand, often noticeable as they are perched on rocks in lakes, or in flocks on sandspits and shellbanks by the sea and sometimes on tree branches overhanging water. Black shags are very nervous of being approached, as fishermen, concerned about competition with the birds in catching trout, have shot them at times.

From a distance they appear black, but in sunlight the feathers are revealed as coppery-bronze edged with black. The colours of their webbed feet indicate the habitats frequented by the various shags. For instance, solely marine-dwelling shags have pink or yellow-coloured feet but black shags have black webbed feet, as they fish in fresh water as well as marine water. Their flight is strong, with wing beats alternating with glides.

Black shags feed on live fish, eels and crustaceans. They usually feed alone but, especially if there is an abundance of fish, the birds are likely to flock together. They do not dive from a height, but from the surface appear to slide into the water, rather than dive, remaining submerged for 30 to 40 seconds. The catch is brought to the surface where it is juggled about so it can be swallowed head-first.

The birds breed throughout New Zealand in small colonies. These sites may be in trees overhanging water, on the ground of small islands in lagoons, or on cliff ledges above inland lakes and rivers. They make large bulky nests from sticks, sometimes also using flax and leaves. Black shags breed during many months of the year, laying three or four eggs and feeding chicks on regurgitated seafood.

Historically, fishermen have used the birds in China and Japan in a mutually beneficial way. With rings round their necks, shags sit on the edges of fishing boats at night and the fishermen's lanterns are used to attract fish. Shags dive after the fish and swallow the smaller ones. When larger fish are caught, the birds cannot swallow them due to the constricting rings round their necks, so fishermen take these fish from the shags.

Pied shag

- Widespread on sheltered coasts and inland lakes.
- Locally common.
- Protected.

Length: 81 cm

Scientific Name:
Phalacrocorax varius varius

Maori Name:
Karuhiruhi

Status: Native

Compared to other species of shags, or cormorants as they are also known, pied shags are remarkably tame. These are the second-largest species of shag in New Zealand and are regularly seen in sheltered marine inlets and bays as well as some inland lakes and lagoons.

The birds are distinctive with their long, white throats and underbodies, and black, webbed feet. Like black shags, their dark feathers appear black, but viewed closely, especially when shags have their wings widespread to dry, these feathers are a bronzy-black.

Pied shags eat a variety of fish and crustaceans, including eels and flounder. Flounder are caught in shallow water and sometimes dragged ashore to prevent escape, before being swallowed head-first. The birds frequently fish in shallow waters, swimming along the surface and diving at intervals. They may jump just clear of the water before plunging in, remaining submerged for 20 to 30 seconds. The wings of all cormorants are not waterproof, so the birds are not buoyant like ducks. If their plumage were completely waterproof, they would expend energy to remain submerged, so their semi-waterproof plumage allows them to fish in deeper water. After a session of fishing, shags need to open their wings and dry their feathers in order to fly.

Like black shags, pied shags may breed throughout the year, especially when food is abundant. They nest in colonies in cliffside trees overhanging the coast, such as pohutukawa, pine and southern rata, and in willows that border inland lakes. The birds frequently use these trees for roosting, resulting in the trees soon becoming denuded as shags peck at the leaves and twigs and their caustic droppings scorch the foliage.

They make bulky nests of sticks lined with leaves. These nests are used repeatedly, with the addition of fresh material each season. Their colonies are often shared with smaller shag species. Like most bird species, shags are noisy at nesting time, uttering harsh croaks, squeals and gurgling sounds. They lay three or four eggs and chicks are fed on varieties of regurgitated fish.

Pied shags were thought by fishermen to have been competitors for trout and consequently were illegally shot. However, it is now understood that the birds are not a threat. Some pied shags are accidentally caught in nets, but this has little effect on the population of the birds.

Little shag

■ Widespread throughout New Zealand waterways.

■ Common.

■ Protected.

Length: 56 cm

Scientific Name:
Phalacrocorax melanoleucos brevirostris

Maori Name:
Kawau-paka

Status: Endemic

Because little shags and little black shags may be confused in identification, descriptions of both these birds are included, even though little black shags are commonly seen only in the North Island. Little shags are widespread throughout New Zealand and are easily identified by their short yellow bills and yellow facial skin.

Little shags occupy small inland lakes, coastal bays, sheltered inlets, estuaries, farm streams, dams and wetlands, and in these varieties of waterways the birds feed on fish, eels, crustaceans, aquatic insects, crayfish and frogs. They have stout bills and tend to fish close inshore alone, pursuing prey in shallow water. When crayfish are caught, the birds shake them until their claws drop off. Eels and frogs are caught in narrow ditches and farm ponds.

Rather confusingly, little shags may be seen in various plumage forms and they are sometimes called little pied shags. The varying colour forms of the little shag are: black with a white throat; a pied form showing white throat and breast; and a smudgy form with white throat and white-flecked breast. The plumage in juveniles is sooty-black, and from a distance they might be confused with little black shags.

Their extended breeding season peaks from October to November, with the birds nesting in colonies that often include other shags. Most commonly, nesting colonies are in willows overhanging fresh water or estuaries, but also sited on ledges in river gorges, in pohutukawa trees on sea cliffs, or low bushes on small islands. They lay three or four eggs, with both parents incubating.

Little black shags are often seen in groups, frequenting freshwater lakes, especially in the Rotorua district, and also inhabit sheltered coastal waters.

The birds have an overall glossy black appearance, including long, thin, black bills, black faces and feet, with their eyes a contrasting emerald-green.

They feed on small fish, particularly eels, crustaceans and aquatic insects. Little black shags are known for their habit of fishing in packs, where the birds swim rapidly after shoals of fish. The shags in front dive while the birds at the rear take short, leapfrog flights to dive in turn. After periods of fishing, all shags perch to dry their only partially waterproofed feathers.

Little black shags also breed in colonies, often with little shags, and with similar nesting behaviour.

Spotted shag

Spotted shags are essentially a marine species, frequenting the open sea and rocky coasts throughout New Zealand, and are not seen inland. They are slender birds and of all New Zealand's shags are the most decorative and elegant, with fine, slim bills, strikingly coloured emerald faces, turquoise-rimmed eyes and the yellow, webbed feet of marine shags. The tips of their soft grey back feathers are each spotted with black and they retain these colours through the year, after losing their ornamental breeding plumage.

They are expert divers and may remain submerged for 30 seconds or more, bringing prey to the surface before swallowing it. Like all shags, when the birds have finished fishing, they perch on convenient rocks or cliffs and spread their wings to dry. Also like other shags, they fly low over the water in long lines, making 'smack-smack-smack' sounds before gradually rising higher.

The birds usually hunt far out at sea in deep water but also in bays, inlets, estuaries and sometimes harbours, catching fish and marine crustaceans. They dive directly from the surface of the water, usually making little jumps into the air before plunging into the sea.

Spotted shags develop a breeding plumage with the formation of two silky, black-tufted crests on their foreheads and top of their heads, and are adorned with a profusion of silky white plumes around their necks. The birds make loud grunts and guttural sounds at nest sites, but are otherwise silent. Males attract mates by extending their crests, flapping wings and rapidly vibrating and moving their heads up and down.

They nest as early as May in the north, although nesting times depend on the availability of food. The birds breed in colonies and some of these are densely packed, like the colony on Banks Peninsula, and in others the nests are more scattered, such as the colony at Marlborough Sounds. Colonies are formed on rocky ledges on vertical sea cliffs, and at the mouths of caves. Spotted shags dive for seaweed that they use in building their large nests and also make use of floating debris, nearby ice plants, grass and tussock. Nests are simple structures with material just piled on to convenient ledges. The birds lay three or four eggs and both parents feed the chicks with regurgitated fish. Juveniles can fly at approximately nine weeks.

White-faced heron

White-faced herons are now a common sight throughout the country in marine wetlands, inland marshes and urban parkland, yet 60 years ago they were infrequently seen. The birds are an Australian species and in the 1950s large flocks suddenly appeared in New Zealand, possibly as a result of drought conditions in Australia.

The plaintive, croaking calls of herons as they fly overhead from one feeding ground to another may be our first indication of their presence. Herons fly in a leisurely manner, allowing an easy view of their draping wings and long legs stretched behind them.

They thrive in a variety of rich feeding grounds, taking advantage of both sea and inland waters. Herons stalk their prey by creeping stealthily through tidal lagoons, shallow pools and wetlands, ready to strike whatever may swim near. The birds catch fish and when the prey is caught they grasp it crosswise in their long, sharp bills and toss it around to be swallowed head-first. Herons not only catch fish but also poke about in the mud, or rake it with a foot, and snatch up crabs, shrimps and marine worms.

The birds are often seen in suburban districts, finding earthworms on sodden playing fields and the grassed verges of busy roads. Some birds have even been known to stalk garden pools and take goldfish. In mid-summer, an ample supply of crickets found on farmland pastures provides them with a ready feast, but herons are more likely to be seen fishing along tidal estuaries at the water's edge. Herons also fish at night by the light of the stars or the moon, as they depend on the rise and fall of the sea.

White-faced herons, like other herons, are well equipped to preen slime from their feathers and bill. Patches of powder down are formed from disintegrating feathers on their flanks. After feeding on oily fish, particularly eels, the birds push their bills and heads into this powder, and then remove the slime by using their feet to scratch it off or by wiping their bills on a branch.

In late winter the birds favour tall trees like pines, macrocarpa or large pohutukawa in which they build large loose nests of sticks and twigs and lay two to four eggs. Although safe from predators, the flimsy nests are often dislodged by storms, so birds frequently re-nest, even in summer.

White heron

White herons are cosmopolitan, inhabiting tropical and temperate regions of the world. They are large, conspicuous, solitary birds frequenting shallow lagoons, mangrove swamps, rivers, lakes and swampy paddocks, and are sometimes seen wading through the brackish, slightly salted waters of tidal streams.

The birds feed on fish, frogs, shrimps and invertebrates, and occasionally small mice foraged among tall, marshy grasses. White herons stalk stealthily through water, at times stirring the mud with their long toes and often standing perfectly still until fish come within reach, then they rapidly strike by thrusting their long necks and dagger-like bills to grasp the prey. Small food is swallowed immediately but larger fish are tossed up to be swallowed head-first.

Like all herons, they make use of a powder patch on their flanks to remove fish slime. They place their bills in this patch of disintegrating feathers then use their feet to scrape the slime from their bills.

In flight, white herons are graceful as they lift themselves languidly into the air, with broad, rounded wings flapping slowly downwards, long necks folded back to the shoulders and black legs stretched beyond their tails. Like other herons, the birds sometimes call with harsh, grating croaks during flight.

In August adult birds undergo a change in plumage, most spectacularly with the development of bridal-like, silky white plumes fanned across their backs. Their bills become black and the facial skin green. After the breeding season, the bills return to yellow. Males display to females by extending crests, groaning loudly, bowing, flaring their silky plumes and snapping their bills. They then perform circling flights around the females, and both birds preen each other.

The only known New Zealand white heron nesting location is near Okarito in Westland. They build large nests of sticks, twigs or fern fronds in trees and the crowns of tree-ferns overhanging a stream near the Okarito lagoon. White herons lay three or four eggs and chicks are fed on regurgitated whitebait. After breeding, birds disperse throughout New Zealand.

The Okarito colony is now a reserve and public access is controlled. Observation hides are available to the public, allowing good views of the nesting colony. White herons are not readily seen, but with protection they are increasing. To Maori, the kotuku symbolises everything rare and beautiful.

Reef heron

■ Cosmopolitan. Widespread on isolated rocky shores of Northland, Coromandel, northern South Island.

■ Uncommon.

■ Protected.

Length: 66 cm

Scientific Name: *Egretta sacra sacra*

Maori Name: Matuku-moana

Status: Native

A cosmopolitan species, inhabiting tropical and temperate zones, these secretive herons are widespread through New Zealand, but not common. Choosing haunts on isolated rocky shores, headlands, mangrove estuaries and tidal streams, they are rarely seen inland. The birds are most likely to be noticed on coasts in Northland, the Coromandel Peninsula, the Marlborough Sounds and Kaikoura.

Sometimes referred to as blue herons, reef herons are an overall slate-grey colour and are more stocky than white-faced herons, with heavier bills. During the breeding season, they develop a fine veil of plume feathers across their backs as well as slight head crests that are extended when nesting pairs greet each other.

They tend to hunt alone, moving cautiously along the water's edge searching for small fish, flounder, eels, crabs and molluscs. Feeding stealthily, they hold their bodies in a skulking, crouched posture, with heads fixed horizontally and necks drawn back. Herons catch prey by shooting out their long necks and rapidly jabbing with their sharp bills. When the water is calm and shallow, the birds sometimes fish by standing motionless, adopting an attitude with wings spread like umbrellas to reduce reflections and attract fish.

Reef herons are dependent on the rise and fall of tides for feeding, and they hunt at night as well as during the day. When moving between feeding grounds, herons fly low over rocks and sea with leisurely, downward wing beats.

Often consuming slimy fish such as eels, the birds preen elaborately by first puffing out their feathers and shaking them, then meticulously combing tail and wing feathers with their bills. Like all herons, they possess powder patches on their flanks to remove fish slime from their bills.

Birds nest in solitary pairs in caves, crevices, rock shelves, flax clumps or in hollows under coastal pohutukawa trees. Frequently nests are reused, becoming bulky with additional twigs and seaweed. New nests tend to be flimsy, built with a few twigs and seaweed. They lay two or three eggs in spring and both parents share all aspects of nesting and rearing, with the family staying together for several weeks after chicks have left the nests. Reef herons are generally silent, except at nesting when they utter hoarse, guttural croaks if disturbed. Nesting birds are disturbed by power boats.

Australasian bittern

New Zealand bitterns are similar to the Australian species. They dwell within freshwater wetlands and swamps, among dense rushes surrounding lakes, and the slightly brackish water of some coastal lagoons throughout New Zealand. They are closely related to herons, with the most obvious differences being their cryptic colouring and secretive habits.

Bitterns are solitary hunters, moving silently and furtively through reed stems, their long toes preventing them from sinking into swamp water. The birds are particularly well camouflaged, with their dappled brown and cream colouring mingling with the light filtering through the rushes. When disturbed, they adopt a freeze attitude with bills turned skyward, eyes held horizontally and sometimes they even sway gently, suggesting a quiver of breeze through the reeds.

Birds forage mainly at dawn and dusk, stalking slowly and stealthily, taking high steps through wetlands to feed on frogs, worms, eels, reptiles, aquatic insects, mice and sometimes small birds. When feeding, they hold their heads and necks parallel to the surface, moving heads from side to side, or keeping still for a moment before lunging and swallowing the prey whole, or first battering the prey. Like herons, bitterns possess powder patches that they use for removing fish slime from bills.

If forced to leave cover, the birds clumsily clamour into the air, and with necks folded back they fly low for about 50 metres before plunging again into cover. As well as calling with low, guttural croaks, males make territorial calls that are mournful booms similar to the sounds of foghorns. Females call with liquid, bubbling sounds. Males can be particularly aggressive towards one another, possibly more so in the breeding season.

Bitterns seem to be polygamous in breeding relationships, with the females attending to all nesting duties. From August to mid-January they build nests that are like shallow bowls of reeds and rushes or just scoops of trampled reeds well hidden in dense vegetation or sometimes built in coastal beds of sedge. Females lay three to six eggs and feed the chicks by regurgitation. When approaching nests, bitterns grip reed stems so they can peer cautiously above. After two weeks the chicks are able to wander from the nest, and they can fly after five weeks.

Bird numbers have been markedly reduced by swamp drainage.

Royal spoonbill

- Cosmopolitan. Widespread in estuaries.
- Locally common. Numbers increasing.
- Protected.

Length: 77 cm

Scientific Name: *Platalea regia*

Maori Name: Kotuku-ngutupapa

Status: Native

Usually seen in estuaries, marshes or tidal creeks, these large white birds belong to the family of ibises, and are immediately distinguishable by their long, black, spatulate (spoon-shaped) bills. Royal spoonbills are self-introduced from Australia and began breeding in New Zealand in the early 1940s. They may be seen perched on posts, or in trees near lagoons, around freshwater lakes and on the coast along tidal mudflats.

The birds usually keep together in small flocks when they are feeding, roosting and flying. Their flight is strong and direct and spoonbills, unlike herons, fly with their necks extended, soaring and gliding in wide arcs. At high tide, they sometimes roost with waders, terns, stilts and gulls, especially in traditional wintering grounds, such as the Manawatu Estuary.

With their spatulate bills, food is located by touch, so spoonbills successfully feed in the dark as well as during the day. Their particular manner of feeding is to gradually move forward, sweeping their partly opened bills from side to side in shallow water or across mudflats at the water's edge. In this way they trap small fish, crustaceans, molluscs and marine insects, with the water being filtered out through the serrated edges of their bills. When capturing larger fish, the birds stop and swallow these before continuing with their sweeping action. In freshwater wetlands they catch tadpoles and frogs.

In the breeding season, males and females develop thick, drooping white plumes at the back of their heads, which they use in courtship display. From October to January a few pairs gather at Okarito, nesting in trees near the white heron colony, and a large, loose spoonbill colony is located on small islands in the Vernon Lagoons in Marlborough. Other sites have been established in Parengarenga Harbour (Northland) and coastal Otago. Both sexes perform exaggerated bowing movements, with frequent bill clapping and low grunts when greeting each other at the nest sites. Their plumes are raised and lowered before the birds preen each other. At Okarito, nests are built high in the forks of big swamp trees like kahikatea, but in Marlborough, spoonbills nest on sandy ground among scrubby grass. The birds build large, bulky, shallow nests of sticks lined with fine grasses in which they lay three or four eggs. After chicks have left the nests, they remain with their parents for several weeks.

Black swan

■ Widespread on inland and coastal lakes.

■ Abundant.

■ Common.

Length: 120 cm

Scientific Name: *Cygnus atratus*

Status: Introduced

Black swans are probably the most easily recognised of all birds, often seen swimming near the edges of well-known urban lakes or boldly approaching for food handouts, along with geese and ducks. The birds were introduced in the 1860s and have proved very successful, as they are now abundant and widespread throughout New Zealand. They prefer low-lying inland lakes, such as the lakes at Rotorua and Taupo, coastal lakes, lagoons and estuaries, especially Kaipara Harbour and Lake Ellesmere, as well as the tidal waters east of Farewell Spit.

The birds appear an overall black, but each feather is outlined in white and wing feathers are edged with a wide, white band that is only noticeable when the birds spread their wings, or are in flight. Black swans appear rather aloof, floating near the lakeshore, with their heads held high as they draw their profusion of curled tail feathers behind them like flouncing skirts. When they call, it is a far-carrying, musical trumpet of sound, often made during flight, or on the water at night. Other sounds are whistles or harsh threatening hisses if cygnets are approached.

Swans find their food in lakes, taking leaves and shoots of aquatic plants. They feed by dipping their long necks and frequently up-ending, displaying only a ruffle of feathers above the water. The birds pluck leaves from submerged plants in lakes, and in estuaries they feed on eelgrass that they pull from shallow sea water. In urban parks beside large lakes, black swans sometimes graze over the grass, also eating clover.

They have an extended breeding season, more active between July and October, and the birds are very aggressive in defending their territories, whether they are nesting as lone pairs or in colonies. These colonies can be immense, such as the one at Lake Ellesmere, where it stretches along the lakeshore. The nests are built about 100 metres from the lake and the birds use available plant material, particularly rushes, creating bulky piles of stems, with shallow depressions on the top, and line these with down. Single pairs lay four to six eggs, while the females in colonies often form crèches of about 40 chicks that are guarded by a few adults.

Swans moult in autumn, so form loose flocks of thousands of birds on secluded lakes and harbours, notably at Farewell Spit where approximately 10,000 birds mingle.

Canada goose

- Widespread on grasslands near waterways.
- Favour Canterbury, Otago, Hawke's Bay, Waikato.
- Common.

Length: 83 cm

Scientific Name:
Branta canadensis maxima

Status:
Introduced

Canada geese were introduced from North America as game birds in the 1870s. They are now well established in Canterbury and North Otago as well as Hawke's Bay and also in Waikato, with some in Northland. In the Canterbury and Otago locations, birds occupy flat valleys of tussock grasslands that are dotted with ponds.

They are wary birds, always alert as they are still considered game birds, and keep together in flocks out of the breeding season. Especially through the winter, Canada geese flock in large numbers, readily taking flight when approached. The birds fly strongly, in V formations, and when flying at night they can often be heard honking to one another. This is a musical double honk and the birds also keep contact with high-pitched trumpeting calls and hiss if disturbed on breeding grounds. For their autumn moult, birds flock to large inland lakes and others nearer the coast, such as Lake Ellesmere. They often stay at these locations through the winter until September, when the birds return to their breeding sites. Some remain and form nesting sites near these lakes.

Canada geese walk with ease as they graze across pasture grasses, favouring clover, lucerne and brassicas and also feeding on stubble or crops of peas and grain. Where they inhabit pasture near wetlands, the birds will eat wetland and aquatic plants, especially rushes. As they are so wary, one of them usually keeps guard while the others feed. On some agricultural land, the geese have become pests by fouling pasture and damaging crops.

In the South Island, from September to November, birds return to the high country to breed in grassy mountain valley sites near the headwaters of rivers flowing from the Southern Alps, and near high-country lakes. Canada geese form scattered colonies or nest in isolated pairs. Some remain near the lakes where they have overwintered and in the North Island the birds usually form nesting sites near wetland locations. They lay four to eight eggs and are very defensive of nests. With the approach of an intruder the goose on the nest will squat very low, with its neck extended flat along the ground, and this posture, with the bird's colouring, proves a good camouflage. Nests are built of rushes and coarse grass and lined with down. After leaving their nests, young chicks join large crèches, with adults taking turns at guarding them.

Paradise shelduck

Also commonly known as paradise ducks, paradise shelducks have larger bodies than ducks, often being referred to as large, goose-like ducks. However, the birds belong to the shelducks, a separate genus from both ducks and geese. They are birds of open spaces, adapting well to the development of pastureland, and are widespread throughout New Zealand, being particularly noticeable in the high country of the Southern Alps. In these southern regions they are often seen on wide riverbeds or near high-country lakes. In the north, they usually graze across pastureland.

Where pairs of birds feed and nest throughout the year, the birds are very territorial, occupying and defending their chosen locations for life, except for the time they spend at communal moulting sites. Paradise shelducks are always seen in pairs and the contrasting colours of the females and males make them easily identifiable. The heads of females are strikingly white with their bodies a deep chestnut colour, while males are predominantly dark, including their heads.

At the sight of an intruder, paradise shelducks fly off, slowly beating their wings, and calling in wild, trumpeting, goose-like honks. Generally, females call with loud, discordant sounds and males utter guttural 'glink-glink' sounds. When it snows, the birds fly off in goose-like V formations to congregate in flocks on lagoons, and they also gather on small lakes from December to February for the annual moult.

Most commonly, birds are seen grazing across pasture, eating seedheads of grasses, clover and grain as well as insects and earthworms. They also inhabit grassy river flats, lakes and occasionally estuarine mudflats, feeding on aquatic weed in lakes and finding crustaceans and molluscs in estuaries.

July to August is their breeding season, sometimes later in the south, but peaking in October. They build nests in the hollows of fallen trees, burrows in the ground or beneath exposed tree roots, under logs or in dense clumps of tussock. In the north, shelducks sometimes choose holes in old puriri trees. Nests tend to be just scraped depressions or shallow bowls of grasses lined with down, where they lay five to eight eggs. If the female leaves the nest to feed, she first covers the eggs with leaves. Parents keep together, whether feeding or attending to the rearing of the chicks.

Blue duck

- Widespread in alpine river regions of North and South Islands.
- Uncommon.
- Protected.

Length: 53 cm

Scientific Name: *Hymenolaimus malacorhynchos*

Maori Names: Whio, kowhiowhio

Status: Endemic

Blue ducks are sometimes called mountain ducks and are easily recognisable in their habitats. Although they are not common, the birds are widespread in alpine river regions of the North and South Islands, but not found north of the central North Island. They are a unique species and show no obvious relationship to other ducks. Their preferred locations are turbulent, cascading, bush-fringed alpine rivers and streams, banked by gorges. They are seldom seen in open, wide rivers or side creeks.

The birds keep together in pairs, occupying the same territory all year, and are very defensive. Their colouring blends well with the dull light seen in high-banked rivers and boulders, with their white bills only noticeable when they move their heads. Unlike all other ducks, blue ducks can see directly forwards in the manner of hawks. Soft, fleshy edges on their bills serve as protection when feeding on rocks and also assist in filtering food. They do not flock like other ducks, but keep together in family groups for a time, and later form pairs.

Blue ducks can dive well, even in swiftly flowing water, and although they do not fly readily, the birds can fly very quickly, with pairs skimming low over the water together, with short, rapid wing beats. If disturbed, they tend to plunge into swiftly flowing currents of water, bobbing rapidly away, and at other times will flatten themselves on rocks when sighting a predator. Characteristic calls made by males are high-pitched whistles. Females make guttural, rasping calls, especially when disturbed.

Blue ducks generally feed at dawn and dusk and also at night, otherwise remaining hidden during the day among foliage on banks. They readily dive in surging water to obtain much of their food, in particular caddis-fly larvae. In deep water, they dive for aquatic insects and from the surface the birds snatch insects and grubs that fall from overhanging trees. They nibble over boulders for invertebrates, wading and dipping their heads and necks under water.

From August to December the birds make nests near the water, on banks, in small caves and hollow logs, beneath dense vegetation or overhanging rocks on riverbanks. Nests are piles of grasses and small sticks, lined with down, in which they lay four to eight eggs. Soon after hatching, ducklings are able to swim and dive, keeping with their parents for some time.

Mallard

■ Widespread in water habitats.

■ Abundant and common.

Length: 58 cm

Scientific Name:
Anas platyrhynchos platyrhynchos

Status: Introduced

Mallards are the world's most successful dabbling ducks, being introduced here from Europe as game birds in the 1860s. Well-established after 1930, they are now widespread throughout New Zealand, comprising 80 per cent of our dabbling ducks. Mallards occupy water habitats that vary from small ponds, shallow lakes, lagoons, farm stock dams, rivers and mudflat estuaries to ponds in urban parks.

Males (upper photo) have distinctive shimmering emerald, silk-like head colouring, white neck rings, yellow bills, chestnut breasts and curly tails. Females (lower photo) are drab in comparison, being wholly brown-flecked, with metallic bills. Female mallards can be confused with grey ducks, but their faces lack the defined markings of grey ducks and mallards sport purple speculums.

Mallards are most likely to be seen on and around urban ponds, and are quite tame, mixing with other water birds. Males call in quiet whistles, uttering subdued 'guab-guab-guab' notes, with females calling in the familiar, harsh 'quack-quack-quack' sounds. The ducks fly strongly with rapidly beating wings and when taking flight leap from the water with a single spring.

Large flocks congregate on freshwater lakes in December and January, when they moult over a period of three weeks. During the duck-shooting season, mallards take refuge on protected wetlands, especially within urban districts.

The ducks dabble at the water's edge for water plants and seeds, and in shallow rivers and waterways they up-end to take tadpoles, water snails and aquatic insects as well as fruits and seeds of aquatic plants. Mallards graze across waterside grasses, eating clover and seeds from growing plants as well as worms, grubs and snails. They also eat ripening grain crops. Females take more insect food to provide sufficient protein for egg laying.

Pairs form in July and establish territories. From August to January they form simple nest bowls of grasses, lined with down and built close to the water in vegetation, hollow trees or hidden under bushes. They lay 8 to 12 eggs and when ducklings hatch they are soon taken to the water. Some interbreeding occurs between mallards and grey ducks.

Grey ducks (not shown) are less confiding, and are recognised by the black-and-white stripes across their faces, white underwings and green speculums. They favour similar waterways to mallards, and are also seen in alpine tarns. Their diet is similar to mallards. Nests are hidden in vegetation or high in trees.

Grey teal

Grey teal are one of New Zealand's smallest dabbling ducks, with the largest numbers having arrived from Australia in the 1950s. The birds are widespread throughout the country, occupying shallow coastal lakes, freshwater swamps, brackish lagoons and estuaries, where shores offer good vegetation cover. They are well established in the Waikato, Hawke's Bay, Canterbury and Otago, with numbers continuing to increase.

At close quarters, the features of grey teal are obviously different from other ducks. They are smaller than most, with steely helmets on their rounded heads, pale faces with crimson eyes and white throats, and lack facial markings. When in flight, the birds display prominent white triangles on upperwings. Grey teal are agile in flight, able to fly straight upwards when disturbed.

They tend to be nomadic in lifestyle, moving freely between various water locations. Flocks of the birds congregate for late summer moults, remaining together until July, and can be heard chattering constantly. Males give loud, short whistles and females make rapid, rasping 'cack-cack-cack-cack' calls.

The birds are predominantly vegetarian, usually feeding at dusk and dawn. They strip seeds from overhanging plants and sift through mud to find fallen seeds, also dabbling in shallow water for shoots of water plants. Flocks are sometimes seen on mudflats where they take midge larvae, beetles and mosquitoes. On the water surface they nibble for minute organisms and aquatic insects and, at other times, may filter insects as they dabble for aquatic vegetation.

Pairs remain together all year and nest from June to November. Choosing sites that are usually close to the water, in hollows and forks of trees or on the ground in clumps of sedges, they build nest bowls of grasses lined with down. Acclimatisation societies have provided nest boxes in some wetland areas that are readily accepted and used by grey teals. The birds lay 4 to 14 eggs, with only two or three chicks finally fledging, even with males assisting in guarding them. When hatched, ducklings are soon led to water.

Brown teal, dumpy nut-brown ducks with white-rimmed eyes, were once common in wetland locations, but are now endangered. Main populations are now on Great Barrier Island and in Northland, with a few other scattered populations. Feeding at dawn and dusk, the birds remain hidden during the day. Birds adapt well to captivity.

New Zealand scaup

■ Widespread on clear lakes and lagoons of North and South Islands.

■ Uncommon.

■ Protected.

Length: 40 cm

Scientific Name: *Aythya novaeseelandiae*

Maori Name: Papango

Status: Endemic

Also known as black teal, scaup are New Zealand's smallest ducks and only true diving ducks. They were once widely distributed throughout New Zealand, but hunting last century and agricultural development of wetlands have restricted the birds to the bigger, deeper and clear lakes and lagoons of both the North and South Islands. The birds are most commonly seen on the South Island subalpine lakes, the hydro lakes of Waikato and the dune lakes of Northland. They are not seen in shallow wetlands or flowing water.

Scaup are sociable birds, non-aggressive in behaviour and relatively approachable. They may be seen swimming and diving near boat ramps and wharves of lakes, such as the wharf at Queenstown, and in sheltered bays of the lakes at Rotorua and Taupo.

Scaup are easily distinguishable from other ducks by their squat, dark, glossy bodies and the males in particular with their bright yellow eyes, although females are a modest, generally brown colour, including their button-brown eyes. Webbed feet that are large and set well back on their bodies assist the birds in diving, and they spend most of their time on water, moving clumsily on land. Scaup fly low over the water, making rapid wing beats that reveal their white underwings. Calls are usually soft, musical chittering sounds and a series of muted whistles from males.

With very efficient diving skills, the birds are able to dive as deeply as 2 metres and maintain these depths while feeding, by paddling their feet. The dives may last from 15 to 40 seconds. They feed more actively in evenings and early mornings, taking aquatic invertebrates, fish, tadpoles, algae, the seeds and shoots of water plants, and surface insects.

In autumn, scaup are more likely to be seen congregated in flocks and from October to January they pair off. Males perform elaborate courtship displays with bodies extended flat on the water, calling in soft, wheezy whistles and sounds of 'whe-whe'. Groups of the birds often nest close by, forming loose colonies in undergrowth near the water's edge. In sedges and lakeside rushes they build bowl-shaped nests of broken reeds and grasses, luxuriantly lined with down feathers. The female incubates the five to eight eggs, while the male keeps guard. Both parents rear the chicks, and immediately after hatching the ducklings are able to dive and find their own food.

Australasian harrier

Widespread in open country.

Abundant. Common.

Protected.

Length: 55–60 cm

Scientific Name: *Circus approximans*

Maori Name: Kahu

Status: Native

Harriers are often referred to as hawks and are essentially birds of the open country, enjoying an increased habitat with the clearing of land. Although commonly seen throughout New Zealand as they glide above pastureland, hill country, forest margins, tussock land, wetlands and roadsides, they are wary birds.

Their effortless, lazy flight as they soar in slow, methodical circles is the characteristic feature most familiar to us. The birds' wings are held upwards, as they swing and sweep, searching for prey, alternating gliding with wing flapping. Harriers' eyes are yellow in comparison with the deep brown eyes of falcons. It is possible to approximately determine the ages of harriers, as in juveniles the plumage is deep brown, later fading to a generalised buff colour.

Harriers catch prey with their talons but rarely chase birds in the air, relying instead on a method of surprise as they hunt birds and animals on the ground. They wade into shallow water to take fish, frogs and tadpoles, or may be seen perching on posts ready to hunt rabbits, hares, rats or the smaller fare of crickets and grasshoppers, as well as the eggs of ground-nesting birds. Harriers are frequently seen ranging over land bordering roadsides, where they scan for carrion and scavenge road-killed possums, rabbits and birds.

They have a prolonged breeding season and perform spectacular aerial courtship displays called 'sky dances' that tend to be above or near the nest sites. Females may be observed flying in zigzag, spiralling displays, with the birds also soaring and tumbling and making impressive swoops, calling with high-pitched 'kee-a' and 'kee-o' and mewing sounds.

The birds usually begin to nest in August or September and are very secretive. They nest among raupo in swamps, pampas, scrub and tangled fern as well as in wheat fields, building untidy nests of rushes and grasses, lined with feathers. Harriers lay four or five eggs, although only two chicks may survive and at the slightest suggestion of any observation of nests, the adults will desert them. When parents are feeding chicks, males hunt and the adult pair sometimes transfers food by passing in mid-air, with the female flying from the nest to meet the male and turning on her back to receive the prey from the male. In the autumn, harriers sometimes gather at communal roosts in swamp or fern country at dusk.

New Zealand falcon

Falcons, sometimes called bush hawks, are able to fly faster than any other bird in the world. They are raptors, or birds of prey, and in New Zealand include three races that differ minimally. The eastern race inhabits South Island high country, the southern race occupies Fiordland and the bush race is located in Westland forests and the hill country and forests of the North Island, south of the Volcanic Plateau.

New Zealand falcons are versatile in flight, coping with many varieties of habitat, particularly where the use of their short wings and long tails allows them to manoeuvre through forest. The birds fly in spectacular, high-diving swoops at 200 kilometres an hour, also flying at speed just above ground level. They possess acute eyesight, being eight times greater than humans'. Males are smaller but swifter than females and the birds call in a repetitive 'kek-kek-kek' as well as piercing whistles and screams in flight, but also soft mewing when at rest.

Falcons are flesh eaters and fearless predators, taking small and large birds on the wing, and small mammals at speed. Not often seen but a most skilled demonstration of flight is the 'pass', when captured prey is passed in full flight, from the male to the female. The female flies up to meet the male with the two birds flying straight towards each other and at the last second both birds roll outwards, their talons touch and prey is transferred. This occurs during courtship and nesting.

Falcons keep large territories, being very defensive and intolerant of intruders at nest sites. Birds nest on bare, high cliff ledges, in trees and on the ground, laying two to four eggs. Chicks are fed on fresh prey, torn up and fed to them and later dangled for them to seize, as they would do in the wild.

Since 2000 BC in the East, falcons have been used in a sport called falconry, in which birds are trained to hunt from the fist. In Europe and the Middle East falconry became classified with social status and laws allowed particular falcons to be flown according to social rank. Worldwide, falconry continues to be practised, using traditional equipment and much of the mediaeval terminology.

Wingspan Birds of Prey Trust at Rotorua is a superb centre where visitors can see falcons in flying demonstrations, interact with the birds and learn about these raptors.

California quail

Introduced in the 1860s for game purposes, these plump, quaint little birds are widely distributed throughout New Zealand, although they are not so common in locations of high rainfall. They frequent open farmland and scrub, where there are bushes for cover and roosting, and also inhabit riverbed margins and the tussock grasslands of the South Island, occurring from sea level to an altitude of 1880 metres. But we are most likely to catch sight of these little quails in family groups as they scurry along country roadsides or feed near protective bushes, even in urban districts. Their most distinctive feature is the black topknot plume of adults that curls forward like a tassel.

The birds watch alertly from prominent posts, rocks or tree perches for intruders, calling with sharp, clicking 'tek-tek' sounds or alarmed 'whit-whit's. Their characteristic and most frequent calls are clear, triple up-and-down whistles. They can run rapidly and rise and glide in flight, producing rapid, whirring wing beats. They are social birds and in autumn family groups flock with others to form large coveys. The flocking behaviour has advantages in that the birds can more readily locate food and guard against predators.

California quail feed in the early morning and late afternoon, foraging for seeds and insects. They take seeds and sometimes the flowers of grasses, clover, sorrel and broom as well as grain in stubble fields. The birds also eat fruits, berries and shoots and in the hill country drink from small pools.

From September to March, pairs separate from flocks and take up their own territories. The breeding season extends over several months, varying according to the weather. The birds do not build nests, but make rounded depressions lined with dried grasses and stems among long grass and under the cover of scrub, brambles, gorse, bracken, fern or logs. During nesting, quail are very secretive and nests are not easily found, but if discovered, nests are frequently deserted by parents. Nests are also likely to be destroyed by predators and unwittingly by farmers in the cultivation of land. The entire brood hatches within an hour or so, and as soon as chicks are dry they can leave the nests. These young chicks appear little larger than bumblebees and within three to four weeks they are able to fly. Chicks remain with their parents, joining others to form coveys that break up again after winter.

Banded rail

Banded rail were once widely distributed through New Zealand, but have suffered with a loss of wetland habitat and predation. The main populations are now found in coastal regions in Northland, Bay of Plenty, north-west Nelson and Stewart Island. They are often seen in open coastal locations on Great Barrier Island but prefer the protection of dense vegetation that borders many wetlands and estuaries. These areas include mangrove swamps, sedge-covered saltmarshes, dense rushes growing in freshwater wetlands and streams that flow into farmland.

Pairs remain together in territories year after year, emerging into the open usually at dawn and dusk. They are very wary and suspicious, and if disturbed will run for the cover of sheltering foliage. Their high-pitched penetrating squeaks are sometimes heard at dusk and low grunting and growling sounds are made near nest sites. Tape recordings of their calls may lure them, especially the 'quee-quee' and 'swit-swit' sounds. The birds rarely fly, even though they are able to fly well.

Although very secretive, the birds may be seen as they feed among mangroves, if approach is cautious and quiet. Banded rail feed in mornings and evenings, eating a mixed diet of invertebrates, crustaceans and molluscs that includes crabs, snails, worms, beetles and spiders, usually finding these on the mudflats of mangrove inlets after high tide when crabs and snails are easily attainable. They also catch frogs and take flies and midges, often gleaned from foliage, and extract worms from seagrass beds. Their diet includes seeds and fruits found among the sedges and swamps. Family groups of banded rail sometimes forage in areas bordering wetlands, lakes and secluded creeks.

Banded rail have an extended breeding season and in the north this usually begins in August. From September to December the birds lay four or five eggs in nests that are well hidden and frequently built in sedges or rushes near mangrove forests. The nests are formed from grasses or rushes, with bowers of reeds or sedges pulled down over them to conceal them from avian predators. The sooty-coloured chicks are active soon after hatching, leaving the nests and feeding when one day old, although their parents guard them for about 10 weeks.

Banded rail nests are sometimes predated by weka, as well as dogs, cats and rats.

Weka

■ Various habitats on offshore islands, Bay of Islands, Bay of Plenty and Stewart Island.

■ Locally common. Not widespread.

■ Protected.

Length: 53 cm

Scientific Name: *Gallirallus australis*

Status: Endemic

Also known as woodhens, weka are about the size of domestic chickens. They are found throughout New Zealand, but the North Island weka suffered a decline in the north in the 1930s and are now more common on offshore islands, in the Bay of Islands and the Bay of Plenty. The western weka and Stewart Island weka inhabit areas of the South Island. The birds live in a variety of habitats, occupying areas along forest margins, dense shrubbery, swampland, sand dunes and rocky shores as well as the tussock grasslands of high country.

As they possess only very small, rounded wings the birds are flightless and rely on their strong legs and feet for mobility, being able to run rapidly, and even though they are not web-footed, they are able to swim long distances. The birds have a well-developed homing instinct that has been proved when they have traversed 130 kilometres of terrain to reach home, and in another instance when birds swam 900 metres back to an island sanctuary, after being removed because of their predatory habits on ground-nesting birds.

Their usual call is a repeated, drawn-out 'ee-wee' with a rising inflection and at other times weka make sounds that are loud, sharp and whistle-like. The birds may be recognised by shrill double-note calls, often made in the evenings. Weka are sometimes seen running from cover to cover, but if undisturbed they wander about, constantly flicking their tails as they search for food. At campsites they often appear quite tame, approaching inquisitively to scavenge food scraps and sometimes running off with brightly coloured fruit or shiny objects.

The birds have a varied diet, foraging for seeds, fallen fruit, lizards and insects. They are known to kill mice and young rabbits, even invading nests of ground-nesting birds to take eggs or chicks. On the coast they eat sand hoppers and crustaceans, often found among kelp.

Their extended nesting season peaks from September to December and the well-hidden nests are built in thick foliage, under rocks or fallen logs and in burrows. These are composed of dried grasses and lined with leaves, feathers or hair in which two to five eggs are laid. Both parents feed the chicks for 6 to 10 weeks.

Like kiwi, weka suffer predation by feral cats, dogs and stoats, but with eradication of pests in some northern areas, the birds are being re-established.

Pukeko

Pukeko are also known as purple swamphens and are found throughout New Zealand, favouring lowland swamps, rough damp pastures, lake edges, marshy grass fields, roadsides and the banks of ponds in city parks. The birds have benefited from forest clearance, allowing them to extend their feeding and nesting range.

They are brilliantly coloured with prominent royal-blue feathering and glossy red frontal shields that form part of their stout, purposeful beaks. As the birds stride across waterlogged pastures they have a habit of persistently flicking their flouncy white petticoat tails, and they move nimbly as they search for food, spreading their large red feet across watery marshes. Pukeko are sociable, often living in groups of several birds, and are generally approachable as they have become accustomed to the presence of humans picnicking beside pools in urban parks.

In flight, they take off rather clumsily but are able to fly distances. They can swim well and will even perch in trees, in spite of their sprawling feet. The birds call with harsh screeches but also make grunts and clicks and low, musical 'tuk-tuk' sounds.

They feed on vegetable matter, foraging in the open and pulling at shoots, stripping seeds and using their bills to unearth rhizomes and corms. On swampy grass and along roadside ditches they eat clover. Long shoots are often held in one foot, parrot fashion, while they use their bills to tear them apart. Pukeko also feed on aquatic plants and insects, and frogs, and will eat carrion as well as occasionally robbing eggs and chicks from nests.

Although pukeko nest through many months of the year, territorial boundaries are established at the end of winter and nesting is more intense from September to December. They sometimes nest in pairs, or they may nest in communities, with two or more females laying eggs in a nest and the incubation being shared by several birds. Nests are deep bowls of interwoven rushes and grasses, well hidden in foliage and often near water. They lay three to six eggs, but as many as 10 to 15 may be laid in a community of nesting birds. Both parents share in all aspects of nest building and the rearing of chicks. Chicks stay in or around nests for the first few days after hatching and are cared for by their parents, or the group, for up to two months.

South Island takahe

■ Restricted
population in
Fiordland.
Others in
sanctuaries.

■ Rare. Localised.

■ Protected.

Length: 63 cm

Scientific Name:
*Porphyrio mantelli
hochstetteri*

Status: Endemic

Takahe are the world's largest rail and were once wide-spread in New Zealand, but climatic changes and the hunting and predation resulting from human settlement reduced the population so dramatically they were thought to be extinct. In 1948 in the Murchison Mountains of Fiordland, they were rediscovered by Dr Geoffrey Orbell. Approximately 170 birds remain in this area, but numbers fluctuate according to the climate, availability of food and predation. Others live in the protection of island sanctuaries and wildlife parks, with the most notable of these being Tiritiri Matangi Island in the Hauraki Gulf, where takahe are successfully breeding and are easy to see.

The birds share some similarities in appearance with pukeko, but are much larger and have stout, short legs and heavier bills that extend onto the forehead as shields. The plumage of takahe is a more subtle iridescent turquoise than the deep blue of pukeko. As takahe evolved over centuries their bodyweight increased, because they had no need to escape predators or fly to obtain food, so they lost the power of flight. Birds call with a 'coo-eet' or use an alarm note that is a deep 'oomf'. At breeding time, pairs sing in duets, with alternating sounds.

They are completely vegetarian, eating roots, shoots, basal stems of red tussock and fallen berries, with their favourite food being the seeds of snow tussock. In winter, when snow covers the tussock, takahe move into nearby beech forest where they dig for underground fern rhizomes and other roots. When feeding on foliage, the birds usually pull out shoots and stems and, holding these in one foot, chew on the plants, digesting the juices and leaving knots of fibres. They are deprived of an abundance of food because of competition from introduced red deer.

Nutrition is an important factor in successful breeding. From mid-October to December takahe build deep nest bowls of fine grasses and tussock shoots in bowers of tussock clumps. They lay two eggs and parents share incubation, but often only one chick survives. Chicks are fed on tussock and grasses and remain for some time with their parents. However, nesting may be unsuccessful through lack of nutrition or the predation of eggs and chicks by stoats.

Where takahe have been placed in sanctuaries, especially Tiritiri Matangi Island, it is possible to see the sooty-black chicks, as well as adults.

Australian coot

Australian coots are cosmopolitan and self-introduced, and since 1958 have bred on Lake Hayes in the South Island, later expanding to many of the large lakes in the North Island as well as Otago and Canterbury. They belong to the rail family, but are essentially aquatic birds, spending most of their lives on still, clear lakes and lagoons that are preferably bordered with reeds and raupo, rather than swamps or brackish, estuarine waters. The birds are more likely to be seen on the water, usually only coming to land to roost and nest. However, on urban lakes they mingle with ducks and can become quite tame, taking bread and grain. Coots are easily distinguishable from ducks with their prominent white frontal shields, pointed bills and overall sooty colour.

Unlike ducks, coots have distinctive lobe-webbed toes, similar to those of dabchicks. But coots are able to walk more easily on land than dabchicks, as their legs are not set as far back. Their calls are harsh, uttered as single notes or penetrating 'krark' sounds and explosive 'kut' calls. Coots fly strongly and over long distances, often landing and resting on water, and like all birds that spend so much time on the water, they swim well, bobbing their heads back and forth as they move along.

Although they eat invertebrates, the birds are largely vegetarian, feeding on aquatic plants that grow in the lakes. They dive regularly for two or three seconds, with their lobed toes propelling them under water where they pluck bunches of waterweed that they bring to the surface. Here they selectively search the weed for succulent shoots and aquatic insects lodged in the leaves. Coots sometimes forage on grass near the water's edge, looking for grubs and insects.

From August to February they breed on the shores of lakes in the North and South Islands, and are very aggressive to other birds in guarding their territories. They have even been known to attack black swans. Quite close to water, the birds build large nest bowls woven from willow rootlets, reed stems and waterweed, often among rushes, or nests may be built under the cover of willow trees and attached to trailing willow branches. They lay five to seven eggs and both parents rear the chicks. In autumn, coots moult their feathers over a short period of time, gathering together on large lakes.

South Island pied oystercatcher

■ Widespread in North Island estuaries in winter. Breed in South Island.

■ Abundant.

■ Protected.

Length: 46 cm

Scientific Name:
Haematopus ostralegus finschi

Maori Name:
Torea

Status:
Native

Known as sipos (or SIPOs) by many birdwatchers, South Island pied oystercatchers are a subspecies of the pied oystercatchers found in many parts of the world. Small groups or very large flocks of several thousand birds can frequently be seen resting on bleached shellbanks and sandspits in favoured estuaries and bays, particularly through winter months. Their clear, shrill, piping 'kleep kleep' seems to echo through the air as they fly with strong, regular wing beats across estuaries at high tide. When alarmed, birds call with a rapid 'pic pic pic'.

The greatest numbers of these oystercatchers can be seen during winter at Miranda on the Firth of Thames and in the Manukau Harbour. The birds are dramatically coloured in striking black-and-white plumage, with their legs a scarlet-pink and their bills a scarlet-orange. Their distinctive pied colouring should not be confused with the changeable colour patterns of variable oystercatchers.

Pied oystercatchers tend to feed in loose flocks, waiting at the water's edge if the tide is high. They do not catch oysters as their name suggests, but probe with their bills for small fish, molluscs and marine worms, and in pastures find earthworms and grubs. Shellfish are prised open by stabbing with their bills and then twisting to loosen the contents. The birds do not have webbed feet but both adults and chicks can swim short distances from one bank to another.

Except for a few pairs recently breeding in Hawke's Bay and Wairarapa, the majority of birds breed in the South Island. They nest on sites east of the Southern Alps on braided shingle riverbeds, farmland, the fringes of lakes and high country. Oystercatchers perform courtship rituals that involve 'piping dances'. They bow their heads and run with short, quick steps in pairs or trios, calling in excited, high-pitched rising trills that slowly lower then trail away. Ground predators are chased from the territory and aerial intruders are mobbed.

Nests are just shallow scrapes in shingle or earth, lined with twigs and often decorated with tiny stones and chips of shells. From August to October three eggs are laid and the pairs remain together, moving with most oystercatchers to North Island estuaries and beaches during winter months. As they do not breed until at least two years old, young birds usually remain in their winter feeding grounds through a further summer.

Variable oystercatcher

Variable oystercatchers are coastal birds and widespread along the coastlines of the three main islands of New Zealand. Some occur more frequently on rocky coasts and others inhabit sandy beach locations, but they are not found inland. Variable oystercatchers are larger than South Island pied oystercatchers, but are less commonly seen.

They are the only oystercatchers that show plumage variations, with the birds seen in two main plumage phases: either all black or a pied form. In the pied form, they can be distinguished from South Island pied oystercatchers as the white may be smudged with black or the line between black and white is usually blurred. The black form is more common in the South Island, especially on Stewart Island.

Oystercatchers are usually seen in pairs, except during winter when they gather in small flocks of 50 or more. They roost separately from South Island pied oystercatchers, and when approached the birds run rapidly away rather than fly at once. Birds make a 'hu-eep' alarm call and are quiet except for a 'kleep' call in flight. They fly strongly and directly, but do not tend to fly up in flocks. The birds swim well, with chicks swimming as readily as the adults.

Variable oystercatchers feed by surface picking and probing deeply in shallow water, sand and mud to extract marine worms, molluscs, mussels, limpets, crabs and sometimes take small fish. The birds often place molluscs upright in the sand and prise them open to draw out the contents, or they may use their bills to hammer through the shells. Birds have been seen to dig out marine worms and then run to the nearest pool of water to rinse the prey before swallowing it. On coastal farmland the oystercatchers find insects, grubs and worms.

Pairs form territories in spring, with some being defended all year, and oystercatchers perform 'piping dances' similar to the South Island pied oystercatcher, in defence of territorial zones. Nests are saucer scrapes in the sand, lightly decorated with shells or twigs, and on rocky shores nests are formed on sand between rocks. The birds make their nests on sandy ridges, near boulders, against driftwood or partly concealed under dune scrub, and on Stewart Island they nest under rocky overhangs or in shallow caves. From October to December variable oystercatchers lay two or three eggs and chicks are able to leave the nests at two days old, although they remain in the territories.

■ Cosmopolitan.
Widespread on
inland and
coastal water-
ways, except
Fiordland.

■ Common.

■ Protected.

Length: 35 cm

Scientific Name:
*Himantopus
himantopus
leucocephalus*

Maori Name:
Poaka

Status:
Native

Aptly named, conspicuous pied stilts are rather thin and angular-shaped birds. Their black tails and wings are long and pointed, with the wing's shape evident in the birds' swift flight. Most obvious of all are the long, spindly, scarlet legs that give the gentle bird a fragile appearance. The stilts' graceful progressions through shallow water in search of food suggest the posturings of a dancer and, in flight, these long legs trail well beyond the tail, like ribbons on a kite.

Pied stilts are cosmopolitan birds, known in other countries as black-winged stilts. The birds are readily seen throughout New Zealand, in sheltered marine harbours, estuaries, saltmarshes, wetlands, riverbeds, lakesides and flooded pastures, particularly during winter. They have benefited from the creation of wet pastureland.

Pied stilts are waders and have been described as opportunist as they feed and nest alongside and within shallow stretches of water, both coastal and inland, wherever there is a ready supply of food. In tidal waters, birds feed at low tide, both day and night.

In marine pools and estuaries they feed on aquatic insects, sometimes standing motionless as the wind blows tiny organisms across the water's surface, before quickly snatching them. In oozy water, stilts sweep their bills from side to side to capture water insects, and in soft mud they probe for molluscs and crustaceans. Pied stilts can wade more deeply than many wading birds, often plunging their heads under water to grasp prey. On flooded pastures, they find an adequate supply of earthworms and grass grubs.

The birds draw attention with their frequent high-pitched 'yep-yep-yep' calls while feeding, when chasing intruders, and as a desolate sound at night as they migrate from one feeding ground to another.

Pied stilts perform elegant courtship displays, especially when they caress after mating, by momentarily crossing their long, jet-black bills. They nest singly or in small, loose flocks near water, whether these are on shellbanks, sand dunes, along riverbeds, banks of ponds or lagoons, on islands in swamps or on wet pastures. Nests are simple, making use of available sticks, grasses and roots, in which they lay four eggs. Defensive of their nests, stilts run or fly towards intruders, dive-bomb or feign injury to distract attention.

New Zealand dotterel

■ Inhabit coasts north from Bay of Plenty and Raglan. Also Stewart Island.

■ Uncommon.

■ Protected.

Length: 25 cm

Scientific Name:
Charadrius obscurus

Maori Name:
Tuturiwhatu

Status: Endemic

These inconspicuous birds are the colours of the sand and seashells of their beach habitats. They are the largest of the dotterels in New Zealand and are distributed north from the Bay of Plenty and Raglan and also on Stewart Island. In the north they are more likely to be seen on eastern sandy coasts, marine harbours and estuaries, but also on grassy banks along coasts.

New Zealand dotterels are known for their tameness, being readily approachable to within a few metres, except when they are nesting. Their calls are typically reedy 'trrrt' and rolling 'turr' sounds and when disturbed the birds may call in high-pitched 'pweep's, accompanied by head bobbing. They run rapidly, although when feeding they walk and search for food or adopt a 'run-stop-peck' manner also typical of plovers. They feed by picking at the surface on wet sand, often near stream mouths, and by foraging on nearby grass where they find crickets, moths and worms. Usually, though, they are seen pecking at molluscs and crustaceans on the sand, and the crabs they find in the mud are bashed and then eaten in pieces.

In early spring, males in particular develop deep russet-coloured breast feathers. From August to December birds form widely spaced and well-defended nesting territories. In the North Island, dotterels prefer broad expanses of sand, particularly near brackish or flowing fresh water, while on Stewart Island nests are sited on rocky highlands. The nests on the sand or shell-banks are just scrapes, sometimes lined with dried grasses, weed or shells and often near the protection of driftwood or under tufts of marram grass. In the high hills of Stewart Island the birds make hollows in moss or foliage and feed on the mudflats and wet herbfields that are below their nesting colony on the island.

Dotterels lay two or three speckled eggs that are well camouflaged on the sand and among the stony shrubbery of Stewart Island high country. Soon after hatching, chicks are active and able to forage for food. Nests that are set low on shellbanks or the shoreline may be destroyed by spring tides or storms and dotterels often suffer predation by stoats, cats and hedgehogs. Vehicles also damage nests, so fencing offers some protection on certain beach sites.

After breeding, the Stewart Island dotterels sometimes move to marine estuaries and mudflats along the South Island coast.

Banded dotterel

- Widespread on coasts, rivers, Rangipo Desert.
- Abundant
- Protected.

Length: 20 cm

Scientific Name:
Charadrius bicinctus bicinctus

Maori Name:
Tuturiwhatu

Status: Endemic

Banded dotterels are small and chubby and the most abundant and widespread of our dotterels. Because they are adaptable, the birds have benefited from increased feeding locations with the cultivation of farmland, particularly near coasts and rivers. They live on sandy beaches, saltmarshes, riverbeds, lakesides and are also seen on high slopes up to 1800 metres, residing all year in the Rangipo Desert.

The birds are easily noticeable, especially in breeding plumage, with distinctive double breast bands, one black and the other a broader chestnut colour. They can run and fly at speed and their calls are penetrating, especially when warning intruders at nest sites. Birds become agitated and defend their nests by flying towards an intruder, circling and running, making bobbing movements and calling with 'pink' sounds.

Sandy mudflats and estuaries are their main feeding grounds and here they run and stop and peck, much like New Zealand dotterels. They find crustaceans, molluscs, marine worms and flies on the wet sand as well as in saltmarshes. The birds also feed on close-cropped farm pasture and ploughed fields along coasts and riverbeds, where they forage for spiders, caterpillars and worms and sometimes eat small fruits on low foliage. Along stony riverbeds the birds take caddis-flies and mayflies. While roosting on the coast at high tide, banded dotterels form loose flocks and remain on their own, not usually mingling with other roosting birds.

Some birds return to their breeding grounds from mid-July, probably flying by night. The birds nest on sandy coasts, especially near stream or river mouths and in grass paddocks, but favourite sites are shingle riverbeds of the lower North Island and the braided riverbeds in the South Island, especially near Canterbury. Birds also nest in the Rangipo Desert. Males take up the territories, defending them vigorously, circling in butterfly-like flights and calling to attract females. Nests are depressions in the ground, sometimes lined with shells and fragments of foliage. From August to September they lay from two to four mottled eggs and chicks leave nests soon after hatching.

After breeding, adults lose their distinctive bands and may be confused with some of the migrant waders. They form flocks, with some remaining in the South Island and others migrating to coasts in the North Island, or to Tasmania and other coasts in Australia, returning in the breeding season.

Wrybill

Usually called wrybills, these birds are also known as wrybill plovers, and although they nest only in the South Island, most birds migrate to the North Island in winter, forming flocks in wide mudflat estuaries such as the Firth of Thames, Manukau Harbour and Parengarenga Harbour.

The little starling-sized birds are the only birds in the world with the tips of their bills curving to the right. With wings the colour of the river stones among which they breed, and with shell-white breasts, wrybills are well camouflaged on riverbeds as well as mudflats and shellbanks. When roosting they tend to congregate separately from other waders, often standing in a relaxed state on one leg and remaining relatively calm, if approached with caution.

Like all waders that depend on the fall of the tide to expose their feeding grounds, wrybills too must wait on shorelines when the tide rises. Wrybills roost impatiently and may suddenly take flight, rapidly beating their small wings so that they vibrate, and this sunlit mass of quivering birds shimmers like a drift of stars. In flight they call in short, high 'tweep's before landing again at roosting spots, shuffling and murmuring as they settle a little longer.

In the estuaries, wrybills feed on aquatic insects, marine crustaceans and spiders, using their curved bills to effectively extract insects from crevices and under stones. The birds also run rapidly, swinging their bills from side to side in a scything motion to catch marine organisms in shallow pools and ooze. On the South Island riverbeds where they breed, the birds feed on insects and their larvae, especially caddis-flies, found under stones. If flash floods occur in the rivers, wrybills feed along the riverbanks on grass insects.

In June, while they are on northern estuaries, wrybills develop a dark breeding band across their chest that lasts until they moult. In August the birds return to the braided shingle riverbed breeding grounds of Canterbury and Otago where they form very loose colonies. They prefer to avoid the willows, lupins and gorse that have destroyed much of their habitat, choosing to nest on bare shingle banks between protective river stones. Wrybills lay two stone-coloured eggs and the chicks are active soon after hatching, even gathering their own food, although guarded by their parents. The normally approachable adults can be aggressive around their nesting territories.

Spur-winged plover

- **Widespread in open spaces, except Fiordland.**
- **Abundant.**
- **Protected.**

Length: 38 cm

Scientific Name:
Vanellus miles novaehollandiae

Status:
Native

Known also as masked plovers and masked lapwings, spur-winged plovers were self-introduced from Australia in the 1930s, with the first pair breeding at Invercargill Airport in 1932. Since then the birds have expanded through Southland and become common throughout New Zealand. The 'spur' refers to the sharp, yellow spurs on the birds' outer wings at the 'wrist' or shoulder of the wings, and these are used defensively. Bold and alert but wary birds, they will respond with fierce attacks if attacked by harriers.

Spur-winged plovers prefer well-grassed paddocks, arable pastures and sports fields where there is a wide, open outlook, and they are also seen on riverbeds and stony ground. The birds reside near lagoons, lakes and along sheltered coasts and tend to remain nearby or within these suitable, selected territories. Finding farmland and urban parkland to be useful habitats, they sometimes roost on buildings.

After the breeding season the birds form small flocks when feeding and roosting. They are noisy birds, making high-pitched, excitable 'keer-kik-ki-ki-ki' calls and piercing, rattling alarm cries. At night they are known for their loud staccato calls while flying. In winter they perform piping displays with six or seven birds facing one another, upright and with spurs exposed, calling harshly. Then there is silence and the birds retreat. Spur-winged plovers fly with distinctive floppy wing beats.

They feed on a wide variety of invertebrates, including earthworms and insects, as well as crickets and grass grubs. Plovers also eat seeds and feed along the shoreline on molluscs, crustaceans and aquatic insects. When hunting, the birds stalk slowly, shoulders hunched and head forward, and then with sudden short runs they capture their prey.

During the breeding season these birds are very territorial and can be extremely aggressive. They respond to the approach of an intruder by performing distraction displays and, if not successful, will dive and sometimes strike with spurs. Nest sites are chosen from June to late November, and the birds lay three or four eggs. Preferred locations are rough open pasture, flat, wet areas and dry riverbeds. Nests are just simple scrapes in the pasture, scantily lined with strands of grass, preferably near ponds or streams. Chicks are precocial, running and feeding within hours of hatching, but remain near parents for many months.

Red knot

- Widespread on coastlines in summer.
- Common.
- Protected.

Length:
24 cm

Scientific Name:
Calidris canutus rogersi

Maori Name:
Huahou

Status:
Migrant. Native

These migrant Arctic waders are also known as lesser knots. They accompany godwits on the long journey from their Arctic breeding sites to New Zealand and the two species usually feed and mingle together along coastlines through the summer.

Knots (upper photo) are about half the size of godwits, with dumpy bodies, shorter legs and much shorter black bills than godwits. These are the easily identifiable differences between knots and godwits, as both species are similar in colouring and frequently roost and fly together.

When the tide has risen across their feeding grounds, knots fidget and fly up in huge, tightly massed flocks, like low, wind-blown clouds being tossed this way and that, rising and lowering, with the birds calling in throaty 'knut-knut's and twittering 'kew-kew's. After these short exhilarating flights, the tangle of knots lands at different roosts on other shellbanks or shores, still waiting for the tide to go down.

Knots find crustaceans and molluscs at levels of the mudflats that are close to the surface, where the organisms are not so deeply wedged and so are more easily attainable by these short-billed birds. They tend to feed in unison, busily running along and dipping their bills into the soft mud or wet sand and then moving on. Waders, with their differing bill shapes, spread across the mudflats, some probing deeply and others near the surface, so they do not compete with one another for food. In the Arctic, they feed on buds, plant shoots, aquatic worms, mosquito larvae and beetles found on pools of melted snow and along the edges of lagoons.

Knots 'colour up' as other waders do, gaining their nuptial plumage (lower photo) before departing for their Arctic breeding grounds. The bright russet colour they develop is more generalised than godwits and includes their faces and part of their wing feathers. The rusty-red feathers tone with the colours of the tundra vegetation and the birds are plump by late March and eager to return to the Arctic tundra to nest. They share similar nesting sites on the ground to godwits, and face the same dangers of predation by Arctic skuas and foxes.

But not all the birds leave; it is possible to see knots all year in New Zealand as about 5000 of them overwinter in some estuaries and will mingle again with the returning migrants the following summer.

Bar-tailed godwit

■ Widespread on coastlines during summer.

■ Abundant.

■ Protected.

Length: 39 cm

Scientific Name:
Limosa lapponica baueri

Maori Name:
Kuaka

Status:
Migrant. Native

This species is also known as the eastern bar-tailed godwit. In late September migrant waders arrive from the Arctic to spend the summer in New Zealand, including 100,000 bar-tailed godwits, the best known and most numerous of the migrant waders. After flying 14,000 kilometres from eastern Siberia and Alaska, they flock to estuaries, inter-tidal inlets and mudflats along eastern coastlines, from Parengarenga in the north to Stewart Island, and to the western coasts of the North Island. When godwits arrive in New Zealand they are a faded grey colour, lean and anxious to feed. They are noticeable with their long, black legs and long, blackish-pink bills that curve slightly upwards (upper photo).

Expanses of soft mudflats provide a rich source of marine organisms and godwits can often be seen feeding at the edge of the tide. The birds feed rapidly, stabbing for crustaceans and molluscs, probing deeply for marine worms and sometimes putting their heads under water to take floating organisms. Then as the tide rises they roost, waiting for their feeding grounds to be exposed again. During this time the impatient birds jostle and fly in short, circling bursts.

Whether flying, roosting or feeding they keep in flocks, often mixing with other migrant waders and, when in flight, a dense flock of godwits is a spectacular sight. Thousands of birds all rise together, creating a sudden rush of wind, and the rapid beating of their wings forms shivering clouds that swerve and twist in unison. During flight the birds call in clear 'kew-kew's and return to the sand with a flourishing swish of wings, running and chattering excitedly.

In March and April godwits and other waders are ready to return to the Arctic to breed. Now plump and a rich chestnut colour (lower photo), the birds restlessly swirl and circle in practice flights before departing. Like other migrating birds, they fly in a V formation where one bird takes a turn to lead the flock.

As the birds nest on the ground, laying four eggs in shallow scrapes among stunted russet-brown Arctic plants and stubbly grasses, their plumage is some camouflage against the danger of predation by Arctic skuas and foxes.

Many younger godwits do not return, staying in New Zealand until the following season, so birds may be seen all year in certain locations. The best time to closely observe godwits is when the tide has risen and they have been driven to roost near the shore.

Black-backed gull

- **Widespread in mainly coastal areas but also inland to high altitudes.**
- **Abundant.**
- **Protected.**

Length: 60 cm

Scientific Name: *Larus dominicanus dominicanus*

Maori Name: Karoro

Status: Native

Also known as southern black-backed gulls or Dominican gulls, black-backed gulls are the largest gulls in New Zealand and the only ones with black backs. These gulls are common throughout New Zealand, favouring open coasts, harbours, estuaries and rivers. They are also seen inland, sometimes at high altitudes, and are well known in urban localities, especially where there are food scraps or refuse dumps. Black-backed gulls have benefited from human settlement and activities, making use of freshly ploughed farmland, wet pastures, city parks and occupations involving fishing.

They are bold birds, although more wary than red-billed gulls, tending to keep a little distant at picnic spots. Confusingly, juveniles show no resemblance to adults, being uniformly brown-flecked with black bills. They do not develop full adult plumage for three years.

The birds are very noisy as they flock and feed, and if they are disturbed at nesting territories, the gulls circle and call, making rasping 'ga-ga-ga' and 'garw-www' sounds. As well as keeping together in flocks at nesting and when they feed, the birds roost together.

Black-backed gulls are successful because they are opportunist and adaptable in their feeding habits and are well-known scavengers, frequently following fishing vessels to snatch offal thrown overboard. They eat a wide range of shellfish, crustaceans, molluscs, worms and insects. The birds often plunge-dive for small fish and marine invertebrates, also carrying shellfish to a height of approximately 20 metres before dropping them to break the shell. The gulls tidy the shore by scavenging on dead birds and other carrion, but also predate the eggs of ground-nesting birds. During stormy weather they often move inland to parks and pasture, where they find worms and insects, and on farmland in the lambing season they are known to feed on sheep placentae.

In the breeding season, from October to December, most pairs nest in large, loose colonies near the seashore, on coastal sand dunes, boulder banks, sandspits and rocky islets. Others nest in isolation on rocky headlands and inland on riverbeds as well as on mountainsides. Due to their familiarity with humans, birds readily nest on buildings near the sea. Nests, in which the gulls lay two or three eggs, are composed of grasses, seaweed, twigs and feathers. After leaving the nests, chicks remain with their parents for several months.

Red-billed gull

■ Widespread in coastal areas and urban harbours.

■ Abundant.

■ Protected.

Length: 37 cm

Scientific Name:
Larus novaehollandiae scopulinus

Maori Names:
Tarapunga, akiaki

Status: Native

The most conspicuous and common gulls seen around the New Zealand coastline are red-billed gulls. They have been dubbed the 'picnic gulls' and will readily approach any food handouts in outdoor public eating spots, and often visit urban parks and sportsfields. The birds are opportunists, taking advantage of any edible waste and, like black-backed gulls, are regularly seen circling refuse dumps.

The gulls are attractive, with brilliant red legs, feet, bills and eye rims. Their outer primary feathers are white-tipped and when birds are resting this creates a polka-dot effect at the tail. The birds flock, often in thousands, when roosting, nesting and feeding, calling with high-pitched screeching, clattery 'scrark' and 'kwe-aaar' sounds. Birds are bold and readily associate with humans, especially around the sea and harbours where they often roost on piers, buildings and boats. As much as the sight of red-billed gulls is familiar, so are their repetitive shrill calls, their quarrelling sounds and competitiveness in chasing food scraps.

Red-billed gulls eat small fish, crustaceans and molluscs, and paddle in shallow pools to disturb marine organisms. They take advantage of fishing boats, flocking and snatching as they feed on offal scraps, and will harass other birds, forcing them to drop food. The gulls come into urban locations, especially in stormy weather, and congregate on wet fields where they find worms and insects. They are also known to rob eggs from nearby nests in their colonies, sometimes as a result of territorial struggles.

The birds form densely packed colonies from September to December along the eastern coasts of the North and South Islands. These are sited on shellbanks, sandspits, gravel beaches, rocky stacks and remote beaches, and are sometimes shared with black-billed gulls and white-fronted terns. The largest mainland colony is at Kaikoura in the South Island, where 5000 pairs nest each year. Red-billed gulls sometimes interbreed with black-billed gulls.

They form small mounds from seaweed, sticks, grasses and feathers, moulding shallow depressions on the top in which they lay two or three eggs. There is often severe competition at nesting sites, and birds are very defensive of the small areas around their nests in the colonies. Colonies are usually sited near plankton-rich waters, with birds eating mainly small shoal fish. Chicks are dependent on their parents for a few weeks after leaving the nests.

Black-billed gull

■ Widespread mainly on South Island inland waterways. Coastal during winter.

■ Common.

■ Protected.

Length: 37 cm

Scientific Name:
Larus bulleri

Maori Name:
Tarapunga

Status:
Endemic

Black-billed gulls are found principally in the South Island and differ from the other two gulls in that they inhabit inland freshwater rivers and lakes, migrating to the coast during winter. They prefer locations in sheltered bays and estuaries along the east coast. The birds have benefited from land cultivation and inhabit flooded pastures as well as the parks of coastal towns during storms, often mingling with red-billed gulls.

They are a slimmer build than red-billed gulls, with longer, narrower black bills, black legs and dark eye rims. Like other gulls, they feed, roost and nest in flocks, but unlike the others, black-billed gulls are less aggressive and less confiding in their association with humans. When immature, the gulls' bills and feet have a reddish tinge and could be confused with red-billed gulls. In flight, the black and white pattern on the wings and outer quills shows more white than the red-billed gull, with the outer black wings tipped white in a polka-dot pattern. Their calls are high-pitched but are not as harsh as the screeches from red-billed gulls.

As principally inland birds, the gulls favour freshwater fish and aquatic insects, invertebrates and grubs. They are often seen on arable pastures where the land has been freshly ploughed, exposing worms and grubs, and hover above flowing water to hawk aerial insects. They are not known to predate other birds' nests, and they neither scavenge nor search out refuse dumps. On the coasts they eat crustaceans, molluscs and small fish.

Black-billed gulls have traditionally nested in large colonies on the shores of inland lakes and along braided shingle riverbeds in the South Island. Often the nests are on islands between two streams. The largest colonies remain in the South Island, with other colonies having formed in the North Island, in particular on the shores of Lake Rotorua, and at Miranda in the Firth of Thames.

The birds lay two or three eggs in their substantial, deep nest mounds that they build with sticks and dried seaweed, and line with grasses. Both parents assist in rearing the chicks and, at about 10 days, the chicks congregate to form crèches that are guarded by a few adults. These are usually situated near the water's edge so chicks can flee to the water if needing to escape a ground predator. The juveniles accompany their parents for many months.

Black-fronted tern

■ Widespread, mainly in South Island inland riverbeds. Many migrate to coast after nesting.

■ Common.

■ Protected.

Length: 29 cm

Scientific Name: *Sterna albostriata*

Maori Name: Tarapiroe

Status: Endemic

Found only in New Zealand, these small terns are commonly seen on or near riverbeds located east of the Alps in the South Island. The birds breed only in the South Island and after nesting many migrate to coastal estuaries and fields, lagoons, harbours and river mouths, with some moving to the North Island. Black-fronted terns rarely venture far from water, whether these are rivers, coasts or wet pastures.

They are smaller and their wings more dusty-grey than both the Caspian and white-fronted terns, and prominent features are their bright orange bills and feet. Their typical monk-like black caps become mottled white in winter.

Their usual call is a repetitive 'kit-kit-kit', especially in flight. They tend to feed silently but will sometimes call in a quiet, extended 'ki-ki-ki-kew' if others are feeding nearby. The birds fly delicately, butterfly-like, as they dip and rise and flicker across the water in search of insects.

Black-fronted terns find abundant food along the braided riverbeds where they nest, not only from the rivers but also in freshly ploughed arable fields nearby where they pick up grass grubs, insects, beetles and worms. During the breeding season, they frequently feed in flocks, working rapidly over flowing rivers, daintily touching their bills on the surface of the water to scoop up nymph mayflies and stoneflies. At other times they fly above the rivers to snatch insects and flies in the air or plunge-dive to take small fish. After dispersing to estuaries and coastal locations in winter, they feed on zooplankton, crustaceans and small fish.

The terns perform elegant aerial courtship displays before nesting on the shingle riverbeds of the eastern South Island and southern Nelson. They form small colonies of up to 50 pairs, with the nests spaced well apart. Often set near boulders or river stones, nests are just shallow scrapes in the shingle, lined with twigs. From October to December they lay two eggs, and soon after hatching the chicks wander about, and can fly at four and a half weeks. If intruders approach the nesting colonies, the terns call harshly, may dive-bomb and even strike with their feet.

Some colony sites are being reduced by a wilderness growth of willows and lupins, and nests are vulnerable to flooding as well as predation by stoats, feral cats and harriers.

Caspian tern

■ Cosmopolitan. Widespread throughout coastal New Zealand.

■ Uncommon.

■ Protected.

Length: 51 cm

Scientific Name: *Sterna caspia*

Maori Name: Tara-nui

Status: Native

Caspian terns are a cosmopolitan species and the world's largest terns. In New Zealand they are seen in estuaries, shallow coastal waters, lagoons, sheltered harbours, mudflats, sandspits and wide, sandy beaches. Although sociable, Caspian terns feed on their own, sometimes on inland lakes, along tidal creeks and major rivers that reach into the high country. The birds are unmistakeable, with stocky, gull-like bodies, sturdy, scarlet bills and sickle-shaped wings.

Like other terns they wear black, monk-like caps, and in winter these are also flecked with white, giving a grey appearance. A noticeable feature is their strong, purposeful flight while calling with raucous 'karh-kaa' sounds. Their calls tend to be harsh, with repeated 'kuk-kuk-kuk's at intruders and rattling 'ra,ra,ra,ra's. At high tide the birds sometimes roost on sandspits with other terns and gulls.

They fish reasonably close to the shore, flying 5 to 10 metres above the surface of the water with bills pointed downwards. They eat only live fish and will fly over swimming shoals of sprats, diving at steep angles and making clumsy splashes as they capture their prey. The terns also catch piper and smaller fish by making shallow plunges near the shore. They sometimes fish alone along estuaries or on inland lakes, where they take small eels, trout and carp.

Caspian terns usually breed in large, loose colonies, but some choose to nest as lone pairs in isolation on secluded headlands, shellspits or the shores of lakes. Colonies may include 20 to 200 pairs and are located on sandy beaches, sand dunes and spits close to shallow salt or brackish water, as well as inland on shingle riverbeds. The main colonies are in Te Arai Point (North Auckland), Kaipara Harbour, Tauranga Harbour, Farewell Spit, Lake Ellesmere and Invercargill Estuary. Groups of terns nest on other sandy beaches and harbours.

The breeding season extends from September to December and courting males bring fish to the chosen nest sites as invitations to females. The nests are shallow, unlined hollows in the sand or shingle, sometimes near driftwood or stunted plants. They lay one to three eggs and chicks are fed fresh fish from the start, offered from the parent's bill (upper photo). Chicks remain at nest sites for five or six days and continue to be fed by parents for several months.

Colony sites are adversely affected by plantings of marram grass and disturbance by dogs and vehicles, so some protection is now in place.

White-fronted tern

Sometimes described as sea swallows, white-fronted terns are the most common of New Zealand's terns. They occupy many seashore habitats, including cliffs, shellbanks, rocky headlands, harbours, estuaries and beaches and are rarely recorded inland. In these coastal locations, white-fronted terns sometimes mingle with other terns and gulls at high-tide roosts and these terns are the ones often seen perched on wharves.

Identifiable markings on these dainty birds are their elongated black, monk-like caps, deeply forked tails and jet-black bills and feet. The terns fly in a graceful, spirited manner, often hovering over feeding and nesting sites before landing. They commonly call with sharp, rolling 'krrrrik' sounds and in flight cry in high-pitched, repeated 'zitt-zitt's followed by rasping 'kee-eet's.

In their exclusively marine diet, terns take small fish like pilchards, anchovies, piper and shrimps, capturing these by plunge-diving from a hovering flight a few metres above the surface of the sea, and when large shoals of fish are apparent near the sea surface they join gulls, gannets and shearwaters. While white-fronted terns hover over a shoal, they twist and turn rapidly in the air before dropping down and, with scarcely a splash, pick their prey from the surface. The birds often forage alone, just above the sea, and will fish in a surge of breaking waves. Particularly in summer, Arctic skuas may pursue the terns, forcing them to disgorge the fish they have just caught.

From October to February white-fronted terns usually breed in tightly packed nesting colonies along the coastlines, sited on shingle or rock shelves, sandy beaches, dunes, shellbanks and steep cliffs. Pair bonds are formed for many years and pairs tend to return to the colonies where they were born. The nests are set on bare ground, sometimes among tufts of sand vegetation, and one or two eggs are laid, producing peppery-sand-coloured chicks. Adults continue to feed the young for about three months after leaving the colony.

At nesting colonies, terns do not keep a low profile if approached but call excitedly and harshly, often hovering overhead and betraying their presence. It is important to be aware of the disturbance to terns if nesting colonies are intruded upon and the birds will settle down if observed from a distance. Adult terns also suffer from predation by cats, and both eggs and chicks are affected by attacks from cats and rats.

New Zealand pigeon

■ **Widespread in forest and scrub, except pure beech forest.**

■ **Common.**

■ **Protected.**

Length: 51 cm

Scientific Name:
Hemiphaga novaseelandiae novaseelandiae

Maori Names:
Kereru, kukupa

Status: Endemic

New Zealand pigeons, adorned in iridescent greeny-mauve and flashing ruby bright eyes, feet and bills, belong to the family of fruit pigeons. They are found throughout New Zealand and are also known as kereru, but are frequently and incorrectly called wood pigeons. The birds are located in mixed forests as well as in open country where there are nearby 'food trees'. However, native pigeons do not inhabit pure beech forest, due to its lack of fruiting trees.

Their rounded wings assist flight through forest trees, with the heavy wing beats producing low, whistling-wind sounds. These magnificent pigeons are sometimes seen flying vertically upwards, stalling and then diving into foliage. These joyous flights are seen throughout the year, particularly near breeding time. Calls are subdued, often low, 'kuu-kuu' sounds if disturbed or when feeding or resting. Unlike most pigeons, native pigeons usually feed and roost alone.

As they seek fruit and flowering trees in open country and gardens, the birds are often seen sweeping low with a characteristic 'swish' before clambering among foliage. Being large and heavy, their clumsy movements lower and rustle the branches as they feed, and they are then vulnerable to predators.

They fly long distances to find adequate sources of fruits, foliage, buds, flowers and leaves, usually gathering them from trees, not the ground. The birds particularly favour the fruit of podocarp trees and are the only birds able to swallow the large fruits of native karaka and puriri trees. They also feed on the foliage of coprosma, kowhai flowers, tree lucerne, the flowers of broom and clover, and the buds of willow and elm. Native pigeons are vitally important in the dispersal of large seeds, as they swallow these fruits whole and uncrushed, then defecate intact seeds over a wide area. They are sometimes seen on islands foraging on coastal muehlenbeckia vines or drinking from pools and streams.

Breeding displays are variations of flight soaring, body bobbing, male posturing and low calls. From September to March the birds breed, building flimsy, shallow nests of thin twigs in native trees and dense foliage, well shaded from the sun. They lay one egg and the chick is fed on regurgitated 'pigeon milk', a protein-rich secretion from the parent's crop, followed later by fruit pulp.

Although protected, New Zealand pigeons continue to be hunted illegally in certain forests and face dangers from stoats, rats and possums.

Rock pigeon

■ Cosmopolitan. Widespread in rural and urban areas.

■ Common.

Length: 33 cm

Scientific Name: *Columba livia*

Status: Introduced

Early European settlers brought pigeons to New Zealand and soon feral populations were established in both rural and urban localities. Cosmopolitan rock pigeons, also known as feral pigeons, are the most sociable of birds and are usually seen as busy, clamouring flocks in parks and city streets where high roof ledges provide safe roosting and food scraps are useful nutriment. Pigeons chase after these scraps, but their natural diet is a variety of seeds and kernels and sometimes fallen fruit. Their unique method of drinking is to suck up water in a continuous draught.

For 5000 years pigeons have associated with humans, since the Egyptians built tall towers to house thousands of them, using the young as a source of food and pigeon droppings as a rich fertiliser. Realising their strong homing instincts, Egyptians used pigeons to carry messages, and pigeon culture spread to Iran, Turkey, Greece and most of Europe. For many centuries pigeons continued to carry messages. In New Zealand, from 1897 to 1908 a pigeon-gram service operated from Great Barrier Island to Auckland, and has recently been revived.

Generally grey with iridescent neck feathers, rock pigeons walk briskly, rapidly nodding their heads forward for efficient vision. They communicate with courtier-like head bobbing, and males in particular produce variations of tuneful coos. In courtship, males circle and bow with necks puffed, strutting pompously with wings outstretched like capes. Once birds are paired, they keep together and are mutually attentive. Pigeons make territorial threat displays by inflating their necks, chasing and using wings to strike. Being sociable birds, they often forage together on the ground and fly in tight, swooping flocks, their wings whacking the air to gain height before quickening to the hum of fluted wind.

Rock pigeons usually nest throughout the year, forming simple structures from sticks and stray feathers in caves, on cliffside ledges or building ledges. The two chicks are fed first on 'pigeon milk' secreted by parents from their crops, then seed pulp.

Worldwide, pigeons continue to live in close contact with humans, many being housed in lofts and used for racing, in shows or as garden pets. When raced, pigeons can fly from Invercargill to Auckland in two days. Wide varieties of colour strains and breeds have been produced. Seen by some as a pest, these birds have a close and valuable relationship with humans.

Kakapo

- Confined to southern offshore sanctuaries.
- Rare.
- Highly endangered; protected.

Length: 63 cm

Scientific Name: *Strigops habroptilus*

Status: Endemic

Sometimes called owl parrots, kakapo are the most highly endangered birds in New Zealand and although scarcely seen by the public, they are unique in the world. A hundred years ago they were widespread, especially in the beech forests of the South Island. They are now rare, with their future depending on successful, controlled breeding on a few predator-free islands in the far south.

They are the largest and only flightless parrots in the world and as well as being nocturnal, solitary birds, they are the only parrots with flat, owl-like faces. Birds walk rather than hop and create well-worn trails through the bush and tussock, using their minimal wings at times to balance when they jump. After roosting in dense cover during the day, kakapo come out at night to feed.

The birds are vegetarian, using their powerful bills to crush and grind foliage and seeds and they also eat fruits, moss and roots found among the subalpine scrub. They characteristically chew grasses, particularly snow tussock, by munching on the leaves while they are still attached to the plants. This leaves fibrous balls hanging on the plant stems and is a reliable indication of the birds' presence. In feeding, they also use their feet to hold food to their bills.

Another unique feature of the birds' behaviour is their use of a 'lek' system in breeding. The males create bowls or shallow depressions from which they call to females in the breeding season from November to February. These bowls, also called courts or arenas, are kept meticulously clean in preparation for courtship and the males' breeding displays at night. In the lek system of breeding, no pair bond is established.

The deep, booming calls of the males begin with short grunts like muffled drums and these increase in volume to a series of echoing booms. Other sounds may be croaks, screams, mews and metallic 'ching's. While males boom, they rock, walk backwards and slowly extend and flap their wings. After mating, females complete all the nesting on their own: forming nest scrapes in hollows, under tussock or logs and sometimes lining these with leaves, feathers and wood dust. They lay two or three eggs, and chicks are fed on regurgitated vegetable matter.

No birds remain on mainland New Zealand and in spite of recent success in assisted breeding, kakapo remain highly endangered.

Kaka

- **Widespread in mature forest throughout New Zealand.**
- **Locally common.**
- **Protected.**

Length:
45 cm

Scientific Name:
Nestor meridionalis

Status:
Endemic

Kaka are plump, richly red-bronze parrots, with stout, hooked bills and strong, agile feet. They are at home in the depths of the forest, surviving best where there are extensive tracts of mature native trees. The birds are strong fliers, able to cross several kilometres from forested offshore islands to the mainland.

They prefer to feed in the upper canopy of forests and the first indication of their presence is often a harsh rattling screech, or falling scraps of bark. In response to a loud whistle, one or two birds may venture from the treetops to investigate, uttering shrill, grating calls. Kaka enjoy their domain and, in contrast to their harsh cries, often call in melodious warbling whistles and trills, flaunting their crimson underwings as they jump and tumble through the branches and tall trees of the forest.

The birds are well equipped to feed on varieties of fruit, succulent shoots and insects. Similar to caged parrots, kaka can grip fruit with two toes and raise a foot to their bills to feed. They rip the bark off rotting wood with their hooked bills to expose hidden insects and succulent huhu grubs and use their brush-tipped tongues to sip honeydew from the bark of beech trees. The birds also extract nectar from the flowers of kowhai, flax, fuchsia, rata and pohutukawa, and ringbark certain trees to tap into the sap. In Northland forests they will crack open the cones of kauri to take out the seeds.

Kaka require deep, dry cavities of large mature trees in which to build their nests, laying three or four eggs on dry beds of soft, powdery wood dust. The male is attentive in collecting food during incubation, and with a gentle warbling he calls the female from the nest, feeding her by regurgitating vegetable matter. The female crouches, quivering her wings as she takes the food. The male also brings food to the chicks.

One of the kaka's most dangerous predators is the stoat, which will enter nesting holes to take eggs and even kill the incubating female. In regions where stoat controls have been enforced there have been remarkable increases in successful nesting.

Although kaka may feed away from the forest, they require nesting sites found only in mature forest trees. The birds are dependent on the protection of these forests for their survival.

Kea

- Inhabit South Island high country and alps.

- Locally common.

- Protected.

Length: 46 cm

Scientific Name: *Nestor notabilis*

Status: Endemic

Kea are the only alpine parrots in the world and have been described as the alpine cousins of kaka. Strictly South Island birds, they occupy high-country forests, steep valleys and mountains, occasionally descending to lower valleys. Although the birds may be seen on river flats, they are a more familiar sight in the alpine basins.

Their olive-green feathers are edged with black, giving the plumage a scaly appearance with the underwing feathers flashing a vivid scarlet when the birds are seen in flight. Their bills are noticeably slimmer and more deeply hooked than kaka, as kea tend to find most of their food by foraging on the ground. Kea are playful, inquisitive birds, unafraid of humans as they snow slide down hut roofs, pull at car windscreen wipers, investigate the interiors and contents of ski huts and adeptly untie shoelaces. In fact they are sometimes called the 'clown' birds.

Kea fly strongly, calling in a shrill, echoing 'keee-aa' as they soar high, often into swirling mountain mists, and seem to delight in tumbling and playing on gusty air currents. At other times, on the ground, the birds call in soft murmurings and whistles.

Like other parrots, kea feed on seeds, foliage, insects and nectar. But with their sharp, hooked bills they also dig out roots and grubs in the ground as well as eat snowberries and the seeds from beech trees. Their hooked bills are useful too when they feed on carrion and if they attack sickly sheep. The birds have learned to rummage through the scraps left in rubbish bins, and their survival may depend on this inventiveness in seeking new food. As they feed on seeds, kea are valuable in dispersing the seeds of the trees and plants that grow in the high country.

They build their nests under logs, rocks and tree roots or in cavities among boulders, sometimes constructing them over several years. Or, after building a nest, they may leave it unused until a following season. The birds form their nests from sticks, grasses, moss and lichens and from July to January they lay two to four eggs, with chicks continuing to be fed by the parents for a few months. Juvenile birds do not breed until they are about three years of age and they are recognised by their yellow ceres and eye rings.

Eastern rosella

■ Found throughout North Island (mainly) and Otago.

■ Locally common.

Length: 32 cm

Scientific Name: *Platycercus eximius*

Status: Introduced

Eastern rosellas, also known as rosella parakeets, are as brilliantly coloured as tropical flowers and are unmistakeable, contrasting with the more subdued tones of many New Zealand birds. They may be self-introduced from Australia, or, more probably, the population has become established from escaped cage birds. Although located in areas throughout New Zealand, eastern rosellas are more commonly seen in the North Island and the Otago region.

They are wary birds and prefer forested habitats or open country with the shelter of trees or forest close by, but frequently visit orchards and gardens, especially when seeds, fruit and berries are available. During winter they are often seen in pairs and will regularly return to favoured feeding sites in gardens and orchards. But the birds move about in groups as well, making their presence obvious with whistles and excited high-pitched, trilling, budgie-like chatter as they approach feeding sites. Often they appear in gardens after fruit has fallen, when only the dried seeds remain on the ground.

Their normal flight is rapid and direct but, when feeding, the birds move in an undulating flight low to the ground and then glide upward to the protection of trees. They call with two-note or three-note whistles or a screech when alarmed, as well as chattering and muted babbling sounds often made while they rummage for seeds on the ground.

Rosellas feed on a wide range of fruits, buds, shoots, seeds and flowers, foraging on the ground as well as feeding in trees. In open country they sometimes take seeds from scotch thistles, and can cause damage in orchards by selectively feeding on new shoots and buds as well as fruit. They occasionally eat insects, such as case moths, especially when nesting. The birds move in a rather gentle and deliberate manner as they feed on the ground, dipping their heads to take fallen seeds, rather than pecking rapidly, and using their feet in slow, careful movements as they scrape among ground litter, almost as though filmed in slow motion.

The breeding season is between October and January and males display by drooping their wings, fluffing feathers and moving their tails from side to side. The birds nest in cavities in trees or dead tree-fern trunks on beds of wood dust, laying from four to six eggs. Both parents rear the chicks and families remain together for several months.

Red-crowned parakeet

- Inhabit mainly offshore islands.
- Locally common.
- Protected.

Length: 28 cm

Scientific Name:
Cyanoramphus novaezelandiae novaezelandiae

Maori Name:
Kakariki

Status: Endemic

Red-crowned parakeets are forest birds favouring lowland native forests, and are commonly known by their Maori name, kakariki. They are sparsely populated on the mainland now, apart from some dense North Island forests, and are more readily seen on many offshore islands. Their bright leafy-green colour conceals them when feeding in the forest.

They tend to be seen alone or in pairs, although they often form small flocks in autumn and winter. Their flight is strong and rapid, with the birds frequently calling in loud, chattering 'ki-ki-ki-ki's, and while feeding they make musical, babbling sounds. Red-crowned parakeets fly long distances to reach good sources of food or fresh water.

They eat varieties of flowers, buds, fruits, leaves, shoots, nectar and seeds, usually obtaining seeds from flax, sedges, beech, grasses and tussock. The flowers, buds and nectar of flax are especially favoured. The birds spend time foraging on the ground as well as in the trees, where, like other parrots, they can rip out shoots and hold them in one foot while chewing. They also eat invertebrates, particularly during the breeding season.

Parakeets nest from October to January, using ready-made sites in holes of branches and tree trunks. They prefer decaying trees, especially old puriri and pohutukawa, but also nest in cliff or rock crevices, burrows on the ground or among dense vegetation. Nests are not usually lined except where old tree hollows offer beds of wood dust, and a few leaves or feathers may be added.

The birds lay four to nine eggs that are incubated by females and later males also assist in feeding the chicks. Chicks leave the nests at six to seven weeks.

Because red-crowned parakeets often feed on the ground, they are vulnerable to feral cats and stoats, so will only thrive where there is protection.

Yellow-crowned parakeets, also called kakariki, are not as readily seen, particularly as they frequent beech forests, where they feed on seeds, buds, shoots, leaves and invertebrates in the upper canopy of tall trees. The birds prefer tracts of taller forest and scrub and less open ground, as they do not tend to forage for fallen seeds and shoots. They take more insects than red-crowned parakeets. Their calls, flight and breeding behaviour are similar to those of red-crowned parakeets, although they tend to build nests in tree holes that are higher off the ground.

Shining cuckoo

■ Widespread in summer.

■ Common.

■ Protected.

Length: 16 cm

Scientific Name:
Chrysococcyx lucidus lucidus

Maori Name:
Pipiwharauroa

Status: Native. Migrant

Found throughout New Zealand, shining cuckoos migrate to and from the Solomon Islands and the Bismarck Archipelago, arriving in New Zealand each September and leaving the following March. The birds are sparrow-sized and not readily seen, although their presence is soon obvious with the whistling calls that announce their arrival. 'Shining' refers to the iridescent metallic-green sheen of their wings. These cuckoos are found in native forest, pine forest, farmlands, willow trees along waterways and in parks and gardens.

Their calls are the most easily recognisable, being slurred silvery double-note whistles that increase in piercing intensity and end with several downward notes. Calls are repeated many times. They also utter clear 'tsee-ew' sounds when several birds are together in tall trees, and may call at night as they fly overhead. Their flight is swift and direct, being only slightly undulating. The birds are normally solitary in behaviour but tend to flock in small numbers between mid-November and mid-January.

Shining cuckoos are mainly insectivorous, eating hairy caterpillars of the magpie moth that other birds will not, collecting bills full of these and then munching on them for some time before discarding the hairy skins. They also feed among high and low foliage on green caterpillars, crane flies, scale insects, cicadas, spiders and slugs.

Typical of cuckoos, the birds neither build their nests nor rear their young. From October to January they return to the same nesting territories of previous years and take over the nests of grey warblers. Fortunately, grey warblers successfully rear their first clutch before shining cuckoos arrive and predate their second brood by laying one egg in each of many warbler nests. It is not known how the large cuckoos succeed in laying their eggs in warblers' delicate nests. Grey warblers become foster parents to the cuckoo chicks, first incubating the eggs and continuing to feed the chicks even after they have left the nests, with the much larger juvenile cuckoos calling incessantly for food. A number of cuckoos are killed by cats and others are stunned by flying into windows.

Adult shining cuckoos leave New Zealand from February to March, returning to overwinter in the Solomon Islands and the Bismarck Archipelago. When their chicks are well fed, they are ready to leave a month later. These young cuckoos depart alone, following the route instinctively.

Morepork

Moreporks are nocturnal owls, hunting in darkness, and as suggested by Dr Jim Flegg, *'those owls which hunt during darkness are the most sophisticated of all hunters'*. They are essentially forest birds, but have adapted to also live in open country where there is shelter of mature trees. They are found throughout New Zealand, with the moreporks' night call being familiar even in urban parks and gardens.

In colouring and habit, they are easily distinguished from the introduced little owls. Moreporks are more darkly patterned, with round heads, longer tails and rounded wings to aid flight through foliage. They are not usually visible during the day, resting within deep shade. If noticed by small birds, moreporks are often mobbed as the birds, chattering in alarm, try to frighten them off.

At dusk, moreporks emerge to begin hunting. Like all raptors, the birds are alert and motionless, focusing fearlessly ahead in the moment before they swoop. They prey on insects, especially weta, as well as geckos, frogs, mice and small birds. Some insects, such as huhu beetles and moths, often attracted to streetlights, are caught on the wing.

The birds call with the characteristic 'quor-quo, quor-quo', as well as soft, vibrating 'cree-cree's and the mewing and rippling sounds made by males at nest sites. Calls can be heard at times through the night and just before dawn.

Like all owls, moreporks fly rapidly and silently. The upper surface of their flight feathers is velvet-like and each feather is edged with a soft fringe. This velvety fringe effectively muffles the sound of air rushing over the wing in flight. There may be no indication when a morepork flies close by in the night. In *Birds of the Grey Wind*, Edward Armstrong says, *'A moment ago she was not and now she is …'* and that *'she comes with a gossamer softness'*. The silence of their flight means that their approach cannot be heard and they can more easily detect their prey.

For nesting sites, moreporks normally choose dry hollows in trees, clumps of astelia and the forks of pine trees. The only nesting material may be available wood dust or pine needles on which they lay the usual two eggs in late October and November. The male brings food to the female and she holds the prey in one talon, tearing off pieces that she gently feeds to the chicks. Families remain together for several weeks.

Little owl

■ **Widespread in pastoral South Island. Not seen in North Island.**

■ **Locally common.**

Length: 23 cm

Scientific Name: *Athene noctua*

Status: Introduced

Little owls, sometimes mistakenly called German owls, were introduced to New Zealand from Germany between 1906 and 1910 by orchardists in Otago, hoping they would control small birds that were damaging fruit crops. However, it proved that the birds fed more frequently on insects. Little owls are now widespread, preferring the open, drier regions of the South Island agricultural and pastoral country to the North Island, where they are not seen.

Like moreporks, little owls are raptors, but are easily distinguished from moreporks by their rather dumpy bodies, short tails, flat heads, white eyebrows and lighter colouring, well mottled with white. The bouncing, undulating movement of their flight is also distinctive, sometimes being low and rapid and more direct when hunting. Another difference is that they can be seen during the day, either prominently perched on fence posts or telegraph lines as they bask in the sun or sheltering in trees and hedgerows.

The birds feed on insects, spiders, beetles, earthworms, snails and lizards, finding these by foraging on pasture, often walking and running freely across the ground and sometimes scanning roadside verges where their prey has been hit by cars. Although they may feed during the day, little owls more frequently hunt at dawn and dusk when they also catch moths, small birds, mice and frogs in their powerful talons.

Like all owls, the birds are equipped with wings adapted for silent flight, with the soft down that fringes the flight feathers suppressing the sound of wing beats and allowing owls to accurately locate their prey. The large yellow eyes of the owls permit little movement so the birds rotate their heads and bob them to judge distances. They also bob up and down if disturbed or alarmed, sometimes hissing and clattering their bills. They call with a repeated uprising 'gyeek' and mewing sounds, particularly in the evening.

Little owls do not build their own nests, but rely on the availability of hollows in trees, buildings, cliffs, haystacks and even old rabbit burrows. In October the birds choose suitable holes and crevices, not bothering with the addition of nesting material. They lay two to four eggs and the chicks remain with the parents for a few weeks.

As their Latin name implies, little owls were associated with the Greek goddess Athene and known as her emblem.

New Zealand kingfisher

■ Very widespread in many habitats.

■ Common.

■ Protected.

Length: 24 cm

Scientific Name:
Halcyon sancta vagans

Maori Name:
Kotare

Status: Native

Kingfishers are prevalent throughout New Zealand, frequenting many habitats. On the coast they can be seen on sheltered beaches, in estuaries and mangrove swamps and on mudflats. Inland, they are found along the shores of lakes, rivers and streams and in smaller numbers in the forest. They are commonly seen in open country, conspicuously perched on telegraph lines, stumps and fence posts.

Some migration occurs between inland regions and the coast according to seasons and availability of food.

The birds have remarkably keen eyesight, enabling them to spot their quarry from a considerable distance and fly with a rapid direct flight, often gliding for short distances. Kingfishers call in piercing, repetitive four to five-syllable whistles, particularly noticeable in spring. At other times, males call to females with a 'ki-ki-ki-ki' and when together they converse in a subdued, musical 'kreee-kreee'. Their small feet are efficient for perching but not walking, as they land on the ground only to grasp prey.

With their strong, stout bills, the jewel-lit kingfishers take a varied diet of live prey that includes insects, lizards, crabs and mice. The birds make use of vantage points from which they swoop to capture their prey, usually brought back to the perch. When larger prey like small birds or mice is caught, kingfishers batter it for some time before swallowing the prey head-first and whole. They delicately snatch dragonflies from the surface of the water and, like hummingbirds, take insects such as cicadas from foliage without alighting, also using this method when snatching crabs from the mudflats. Kingfishers swoop silently on prey and this, combined with dazzling speed, is most impressive when they dive for fish. The birds perch a few metres above the water's surface, intently watching their prey before making a rapid, shallow dive to grip the fish crosswise in their bills. The time from leaving a low perch, diving and returning to the perch has been recorded as 1.5 to 2 seconds.

In early spring, they choose vertical clay banks, cliffs, knotholes and rotting tree trunks in which both males and females bore tunnels about 20 centimetres long. They lay four to six eggs on bare earth or wood chips and chicks are first fed on insects, then later on lizards and whole fish. However, kingfisher nests are sometimes predated by mynas, which enlarge the clay-bank entrance holes or reach into shorter tunnels and take over the kingfishers' nests.

Rifleman

- More common in South Island beech forest. Also in high-country forests of North Island.
- Locally common.
- Protected.

Length: 8 cm

Scientific Name: *Acanthisitta chloris*

Maori Name: Titipounamu

Status: Endemic

Tiny riflemen are the smallest of New Zealand birds and are widespread in native and exotic forest throughout the country, usually at levels above 400 metres. They are more commonly found in large tracts of high-country beech forests in the South Island but are also reasonably numerous in other high-country forests, including some of the pine forests and adjacent scrublands. In the North Island they occupy high-altitude beech forests in particular, and may be seen in Coromandel, but are infrequent north of Waikato.

Riflemen do not have a tail. A particular feature is the incessant flicking movement of their wings that accompanies their jerky hops through the branches of trees and even continues when the birds are perched. It is considered that the birds were so named because their colouring is suggestive of a soldier's uniform and their tiny upturned beaks rather fancifully appear as the shape of a rifle. The riflemen's call is a rapid, high-frequency 'tsit-tsit' and flight is short and direct, with their fast, flittering flight as they progress through foliage being most distinctive.

The birds are mainly insectivorous and as they feed they are forever moving, with their nimble legs and claws clinging in any attitude on the bark of trees. As they hunt for insects on trees and among foliage, they spiral upwards from the base and flutter around the tree trunks and branches, poking their slightly upcurved bills into moss, lichen and scaling bark. Near the treetops the birds drop down again and repeat the manoeuvre on another tree. They hang upside down, glean in crevices and move rapidly among the foliage, eating insects and their larvae, spiders, moths and beetles. Some ripe fruit is also taken, but the birds rarely feed on the forest floor.

Pairs of the birds remain in their territory all year and begin nesting from September to November. They build their nests in small cavities and knotholes in trees, under flaking bark or among rocks or crevices in cliffs. The birds tuck nesting material into these tiny cavities, weaving together dry grass, fine twigs, moss and rootlets, then line the nests with feathers and soft grasses. Three to four eggs are laid. Both parents feed the chicks on insects, often assisted by older chicks from a previous brood. Riflemen tend to keep within small territories of approximately a square kilometre.

Welcome swallow

- **Widespread in open country throughout New Zealand.**
- **Abundant.**
- **Protected.**

Length:
15 cm

Scientific Name:
Hirundo tahitica neoxena

Status:
Native

Now commonly seen in open country throughout New Zealand, welcome swallows were self-introduced from Australia in the 1950s. As they find most of their insect food near the surface of water, the birds tend to live close to lakes, rivers, swamps and the seashore. They are more likely to be seen in small groups, perched on telephone lines and fences, not only as vantage points but because they find it easier to launch into the air from high perches. From a distance the birds appear to be an overall dark colour, but a close view reveals their deep glossy indigo and chestnut feathers.

They are slender birds with long, pointed wings and distinctively forked tails, enabling them a swift diversity of flight to catch insects on the wing. Swallows are strictly insectivorous birds, circling gracefully and then swooping at full speed to snatch tiny insects, moths and beetles just above the water's surface. This ability to sweep across water also allows them to dip their bills and snatch a drink in mid-flight. In summer evenings and on warm days, the birds sometimes fly higher in the air to take advantage of the flurries of mosquitoes and midges. In winter, swallows often move to the coast, where they hawk the flies that hover over kelp.

Flocks of the birds may congregate, particularly in autumn and winter and especially where there is an abundance of food, keeping contact with high-pitched 'zwitt' sounds and warbling twitters mingled with short, throaty trills. On pastures, they sometimes flit low over sodden grass and puddles, taking grass flies. In sweeping across sewage ponds, flocks of swallows find an abundance of insect food. At night, birds often roost together in raupo beds and rushes or in trees above water.

Courtship involves the male displaying to the female by chasing and tail fanning, then both birds rub beaks. They build rather rough nests of mud and dried grasses, lined with feathers, wool and fibres. These are deep cup-shaped structures cemented to walls of culverts, bridges, ledges of buildings, boats, farm water tanks and shallow depressions in cliffs. Swallows have benefited from the development of land and construction. Both birds help build the nest, darting back and forth with beakfuls of soft mud to bind the grasses and twigs. They lay three to five eggs and both parents feed the chicks.

New Zealand pipit

■ Widespread from sea level to high country.

■ Uncommon.

■ Protected.

Length: 19 cm

Scientific Name:
Anthus novaeseelandiae novaeseelandiae

Maori Name:
Pihoihoi

Status: Endemic

Pipits are sometimes referred to as ground larks and may be confused with the introduced skylarks. Mistaken identity may result from similarities in colour and size. New Zealand pipits are widely distributed throughout the country and have benefited from the clearance of land, although they prefer rough, scrubby pastures and tussock land. In the rocky grasslands of the high country they can be seen at high-altitude herbfields to levels of 2000 metres, and in some regions of tussock they may be the only birds to be seen. Pipits are also located along roadsides, forest margins, riverbeds, estuaries and in coastal locations.

Pipits are more slender than skylarks and do not have crests, but the quickest method of identification is to observe their behaviour. Skylarks are wary but pipits are easily approachable and repetitively flick their tails as they walk, also making a slight dipping motion with each step. The birds spend a lot of time on the ground, often running and rising in short, fluttery flights, whereas skylarks are more frequently seen in flight, singing as they soar higher and higher. Pipits like to sing from prominent perches, calling in high-pitched musical trills, with shrill 'scree' and 'pee-pit' sounds being common. In regard to the walking and running habits, H. Guthrie-Smith observed a pipit's departure as *'little runs and pauses that carry him further and further …'*.

Pipits are almost entirely insectivorous, taking a few seeds. In autumn and winter many birds form loose flocks, feeding together across the ground wherever there is an abundance of insects. They follow freshly ploughed land, picking up beetle larvae and worms, or the birds visit farming sheds to catch disturbed insects. They also eat crickets, moths, flies, wasps, grubs and snails, sometimes catching these by perching on high posts and hawking them. On estuaries and along shorelines they pick delicately at sand hoppers and kelp flies, and on farmland their favoured seeds are grass, clover and thistles.

The birds have an extended breeding season, from September to February. Their nests are deep cups of woven grass, lined with moss, lichen and herbage, and these are built on the ground, well hidden on steep banks beneath tussock or gorse, and among low bracken or tall grasses. They lay three or four eggs, with both parents feeding the chicks on a variety of insects. Some nests suffer predation by magpies.

Blackbird

Blackbirds were introduced in the 1860s by British settlers, as nostalgic reminders of home. They are now commonly found throughout New Zealand, even occupying native forest, where they tend to behave more warily than in the open country. The birds are readily seen in pastureland, gardens and parks, favouring localities where there is some protection of hedges or shrubs.

After their autumn moult, males (upper photo) assume a vivid black colouring with bright orange bills and eye rims. Females (lower photo) are dusky-brown and slightly spotted or streaked; identifying them could be confusing, as they are not black. Males produce the flute-like whistles and calls that begin in spring and, from an elevated perch, they sing in long mellow, rippling notes including clucks and clattering sounds before a trill of clear rippling calls.

The birds eat a variety of invertebrates, including insects, beetles, caterpillars, worms and grubs, and sometimes they range along the shoreline and feed on marine insects. Blackbirds also eat a wide variety of fruit from trees such as native podocarps and nikau palms as well as from shrubs and weeds. In orchards they cause damage to large fruit with their pecking and also spread seeds from weed berries into the forest. When searching for insect food, blackbirds tend to feed near bushes or where there is cover. Insects are also found among leaf litter with the birds flicking aside the leaves with their bills. When hunting for worms, they hop short distances and then stand still, continuing these little runs and pauses until they find a worm, and then quickly pull it out.

Blackbirds tend to use the same nesting territories each year and males defend these sites with frequent threat displays and calls. From July to January the birds build their bulky nests of twigs, roots, moss and leaves, lining them with grasses bound together with a little mud. Nests are set in the forks of trees, or hedges, even on rock and building ledges. The birds lay three to five eggs and both parents feed the chicks. The sight of a blackbird with a bill full of worms would indicate that it has a nest nearby and is feeding chicks.

Blackbirds regularly visit gardens, especially in winter, and are attracted to pieces of fruit, such as apple cores, on bird tables.

Song thrush

■ Widespread
throughout
New Zealand
from sea level to
subalpine scrub.
Not in deep
forest.

■ Abundant.
Common.

Length: 23 cm

Scientific Name:
Turdus philomelos

Status: Introduced

Thrushes were introduced from Europe in the 1860s, at the same time as blackbirds, and soon spread throughout the open country of New Zealand. They are now commonly seen in suburban gardens, parks, scrub and exotic forest habitats that extend from sea level to subalpine scrub. Song thrushes do not enter the depths of the forests, as blackbirds are known to do.

Song thrushes feed on a variety of insects, spiders and worms as well as the small fruit of native shrubs and weeds. They also peck larger orchard fruit, causing damage particularly to grapes, tomatoes and berry fruit. It is common to see thrushes in the garden searching for either worms or snails. The birds progress across the grass by running and in little hopping jumps. They run briefly, and then stand still with heads cocked, appearing to listen, but thrushes are actually looking downward, watching for small movements indicating worms. Then they will jump as they dig into the earth, dragging out the worm and pecking along its body to incapacitate it. Snails are usually found hiding under foliage and the birds have a way of gripping the lip of the shell's opening, finding a convenient stone and hammering the shell till it breaks. Particular stones or pathways become regular anvils for breaking snail shells.

Thrushes begin to sing in the middle of winter, often from high perches, late in the afternoon or at dusk before roosting. These clear musical whistles are repetitions of three-syllable upward notes, a pause and two downward notes. Their alarm call is a hurried 'chuk' sound and in flight they may call in high-pitched 'seeps'.

The birds sometimes breed as early as June in the north, but usually from August to January. Females construct nests from twigs, grasses and moss that are lined with mud, and they build these in the forks of trees or in dense shrubs. They lay four to five eggs and both parents feed the chicks, often with worms and insects.

Like all birds that depend on insects and worms foraged on the ground, particularly in gardens, thrushes may easily become victims of household cats. Perhaps, because of this, they tend to be cautious in their movements and while running along the ground appear alert and defensive. Because they feed readily on snails, the birds are sometimes victims of poisonous slug bait in gardens.

Fernbird

Fernbirds belong to the family of grass warblers, and even though their songs may be restricted to quick whistles and clicks, these sounds are usually the only notable indication of the birds' presence. Although quite widespread throughout New Zealand, with five subspecies, they are secretive in behaviour and not easily seen.

They inhabit the seclusion of the tall grasses, rushes, raupo, reeds and flax of wetlands and marsh sedges as well as the bracken and tussock of drier regions. Within these dense covers the slender birds slip through stealthily. If they can be viewed, the most obvious features are their long fern-like tails, with the disconnected barbs of these tail feathers giving them a loose, wispy appearance.

Among the vegetation that conceals them, the birds feed on insects, caterpillars, grubs, beetles, flies and moths, with the tiny spiders that emerge from the nurseryweb cocoons being a favourite food. They have strong leg bones, developed through their habit of ground foraging, by scurrying through rushes clinging to the stems and perching astride lightweight grasses and flax. Fernbirds climb up foliage in little runs, just like mice.

They have short wings and their flight is weak when forced to leave cover, fluttering low across vegetation with their tails drooped down. Even though the birds are more readily heard than seen, their calls are neither warbling nor distinctive. Pairs maintain contact by calling in duets of a 'u' by the males and immediate 'tick' replies by the females. Calls tend to be metallic and other typical sounds are 'too-lit' and the rapidly repeated 'di,di,di,di' by males when disturbed or alarmed. By calling them with a double whistle, they sometimes approach you to investigate or may perch briefly at the top of swamp rushes.

Both birds of a pair make their nests, which are loose, cup-shaped structures, woven with dried grasses, lined with feathers and concealed in rushes, cutty grass, tussock and sedges. Nests are sometimes built in saltmarsh sedges but these may be flooded by spring tides. They lay three or four eggs and chicks are fed on tiny insects. The juveniles remain dependent on their parents for a few weeks after leaving their nests.

The birds rely on wetland habitats where there is an adequate protective covering of flax and reeds. Fernbirds fly weakly and so cannot adapt easily to changes in their environment caused by drainage and development.

Whitehead

■ Found in North Island only, in forests south of Waikato, and offshore islands.

■ Locally common.

■ Protected.

Length: 15 cm

Scientific Name:
Mohoua albicilla

Maori Names:
Popokatea, tataeko

Status: Endemic

Whiteheads are found in the North Island and are closely related to the yellowheads of the South Island. They are located on Little Barrier and Tiritiri Matangi Islands and south of Waikato, and have recently been introduced to the Waitakere Ranges. They prefer large tracts of forest and are common in native forests, as well as pine forests and scrub.

They are very social birds and are usually seen together in family groups, although whiteheads are more likely to be heard than seen, as they feed noisily in the upper forest canopy. They usually keep together in small flocks most of the year, often joining up with parakeets, saddlebacks and silvereyes to take advantage of an abundance of dislodged insects. The birds are very vocal during the day and through most of the year, calling with repeated 'zwit' or 'chip' sounds. Males make loud territorial calls from prominent perches that consist of rapid, musical chirps followed by canary-like trills.

The birds are active in their search for food, mainly eating invertebrates found by using their bills to flake off bark and break up wood to expose the insects, as well as hanging from branches to glean insects from leaves. They take caterpillars, spiders, beetles and moths and will eat small fruits and seeds from native shrubs and podocarp trees. Whiteheads rarely feed on the ground and are likely to be seen climbing acrobatically about foliage, clinging to tree bark and using their spine-like tails to assist them in climbing.

Whiteheads nest from October to January and are thought to be polygamous, as two females often accompany a male, although these could be a family group from the previous year. They form compact, cup-shaped nests from moss, grass, fragments of bark and leaves bound together with spiders' web, lined with tree-fern scales and feathers. Nests may be built in the forks of trees, such as manuka, or in shrubs. They lay three or four eggs and both parents feed the chicks, assisted by another female and sometimes others. Long-tailed cuckoos use whiteheads to incubate their eggs and rear the large cuckoo chicks.

Yellowheads are located only in the South Island, and their numbers have declined, due to predation by stoats. They are now confined to larger areas of beech forest. Yellowheads are closely related to whiteheads and have similar feeding habits and nesting, although yellowheads choose to nest in shallow cavities of trees in high levels of the forest.

Grey warbler

- Widespread in forests and shrubbery from sea to alpine levels.
- Abundant.
- Protected.

Length: 10 cm

Scientific Name:
Gerygone igata

Maori Name:
Riroriro

Status:
Endemic

Grey warblers are tiny, lively birds seen in most habitats throughout New Zealand from sea to alpine levels, wherever there is forest, scrub, mangrove or thicket. They were originally classified as warblers because they resemble 'old world' species in shape, habit and song. However, they are not related but linked instead to the songbirds. They are frequently seen in gardens and parks, where there is sufficient sheltered shrubbery and where an abundance of insects may lurk.

The birds are likely to be seen in pairs, particularly in the breeding season, as they flitter restlessly, jittering and dancing through the branches as they disturb foliage to find insect food. Their colouring is dull, but noticeable are white edges to their wings as they flicker from tree to tree. Their sweet, lyrical songs, heard throughout the seasons, are high-pitched trilling, tremulous warbles often halted mid-song, as though suddenly interrupted. Then the calls are repeated.

Their bills are thin, typical of insectivorous birds that feed on invertebrates, such as spiders, caterpillars, flies and little beetles. Grey warblers have an advantage in being so light that they can hover momentarily in mid-air, plucking insects from the leaves of outer branches. Sometimes they also eat small, ripe fruit.

In August, grey warblers begin nesting, laying three or four eggs. They favour thickets of manuka and small-leafed trees like kahikatea in which to build their nests. These intricate pear-shaped structures are woven so that they suspend from a branch, sometimes attached at other points to be held securely. Dried grasses, moss, leaves, lichen, wool and shreds of bark are gathered and woven together with silk from spiders' webs. The hanging nests are padded with moss then lined with the softest feathers and thistledown. Entrance to each nest is through a circular opening on the side. It was once noted that where there were fragments of sheep's wool clinging to a farm fence, they were collected by grey warblers to create a snug cushioned nest.

After grey warblers have successfully raised their first brood of chicks, they lay a second brood a few weeks later. At this time, shining cuckoos often take advantage by laying a single egg in some of these nests, leaving the large cuckoo chick to be raised by the warblers, at the expense of warbler chicks.

Fantail

- Widespread in most habitats.
- Abundant.
- Protected.

Length: 16 cm

Scientific Name: *Rhipidura fuliginosa*

Maori name: Piwakawaka

Status: Native

Termed '*this fairy of the bush*' by Guthrie-Smith, fantails are found throughout New Zealand and, although forest birds, they have adapted well to the development of land. The birds are seen in forest, scrub, open country, pine forests and gardens, but are not so common where severe frosts or snow result in a lack of flying insects.

Fantails vary from brown with russet breasts to some being sooty black in the South Island. Their flickering silver-and-black fanned tail feathers are an animated feature that they use constantly in flight, feeding and display. The birds are forever on the move and in flight they may hold their tails loose, then rapidly fan them this way and that, stopping in mid-air to change direction.

Feeding on invertebrates such as insects, flies, moths, wasps, beetles and mosquitoes, fantails usually take these on the wing. The birds use a variety of methods to obtain insect food. They move upside down among and along tree-fern fronds and foliage, taking insects from beneath the leaves or catching them as they fall. Their fanned tails are also used to sweep across foliage to dislodge insects, and birds sometimes mingle with silvereyes, saddlebacks and whiteheads or flutter about people as they walk, to take advantage of insects disturbed by their movements. Fantails also forage among forest leaf litter.

The birds call with simple rhythmical twitters and squeaky chattering, making a penetrating 'cheet' as a contact call. In display, males strut and perform spirited aerial turns and use their tails to flamboyant effect by fanning them widely. When birds pair, they remain together all year, usually retaining territories from past seasons, with the males being very defensive at nesting time and snapping their bills at intruders.

In late August the females build their distinctive tight, circular nest cups from dried grasses, fragments of bark, lichen and moss lined with fern fibres and feathers. Nests are bound together with spiders' webs and woven across narrow branches, leaving frail, tapering tails of nest material trailing from the base. They are set in the forks of shrubbery and fronds of tree-ferns that are near or leaning over a stream. Fantails lay two to four eggs and the growing chicks soon bulge from the small nest cup. After they have left their nest, fledgling fantails may sometimes be seen at dawn, feathers puffed, and cuddled together on a branch.

Tomtit

Tomtits are widely distributed throughout New Zealand and are seen in the forest as well as in tall scrubland. The birds especially favour beech forest in both the North and South Islands. They have adapted well to cleared land and inhabit mature exotic forest, freely entering pine plantations. Pairs will occupy their territories all year, with the birds tending to maintain wide territories, so tomtits may not be seen together in large numbers.

Males (upper photo) are pied, being black with a white breast. Females (lower photo) are brown and the breast plumage is smudged white, so they appear drabber than the males. Males are more inquisitive than females, so are more frequently seen. The males' songs are the more commonly heard, with the birds often calling in high-pitched 'seee-seee' notes and making brief whistling calls. They also sing in low notes and warbling 'yodi-yodi-yodi' tones, usually as forms of communication between pairs. Females will occasionally call in excited warbles, similar to the males, and the birds often sing while feeding.

Tomtits find a variety of insects on tree trunks, branches, foliage and the forest floor. They flit from tree to tree and, clinging sideways, search for insects, including beetles, flies and wasps as well as spiders, worms and moths. They do not scratch on the ground, but make short, rapid flights among the trees, scanning the ground, and when prey is sighted the birds fly down and snatch it. Insects are also gleaned from leaves and branches and in autumn they supplement their diet with small fruits. Although feeding close by, tomtits and robins do not compete for food, as robins tend to feed in lower forest, while tomtits spend more time in the higher canopy.

From August to January they nest, laying three or four eggs. Tomtits form cup-shaped nests that are finely constructed of moss, bark fragments and rootlets bound together with spiders' web and lined with feathers. They are usually difficult to find as the birds hide them in tree-trunk holes, clefts in banks, in the forks of low trees or even under tussock. Favourite sites are the hollows of rotten tree trunks, the sides of tree-fern trunks and in tangles of vines. Both parents feed the chicks and once the juveniles are independent, they soon disperse to other territories.

New Zealand robin

Robins are found throughout New Zealand, with small colour differences between the subspecies. They favour the shade of mature native forests, some exotic forests and tall, dense manuka scrub, with pairs defensively maintaining their territories through the year. Because of land clearance, robins in lowland forests have declined.

They may be drab in plumage but robins are perky birds, with slender black legs, and as they pause on outer branches, the birds watch enquiringly with their glimmering black eyes. Their dull colouring is good camouflage and they are especially difficult to see in forest twilight. However, the birds are confiding and unafraid of humans as they approach close to walkways where forest litter has recently been disturbed and exposed insects are easily spotted.

Robins hop on their dainty feet, rather than walk, plucking insects, worms and grubs from beneath fallen leaves. They take spiders as well as weta, spending more time on the ground foraging for food than tomtits. The birds also search through foliage in undergrowth shrubbery, gleaning insects from leaves and feeding on larger prey such as cicadas and stick insects. Robins move to higher tree branches, and especially during summer they hunt for prey in the upper storey of forests.

Males sing from high perches with outpourings of warbles that rise and fall in volume. Songs begin with a few staccato and rather plaintive notes before bursting into a full, ringing song that lasts without pause for as long as 20 minutes and even up to an hour. The birds fly rapidly and directly through the forest.

The breeding season extends from September to January, with birds laying three or four eggs. They form bulky cup nests from twigs, moss and rootlets bound with spiders' web and lined with tree-fern scales and fine grasses. Nests are built in tree forks, hollows of trees, in the shallow crevices of old trees or the ends of broken branches. Robins nest at a lower level than tomtits. Both parents feed the chicks and continue to care for them for several weeks. To distract intruders from nests, the birds fly close by, then with wings and tails fanned out, spiral to the ground where they slowly pirouette from side to side.

Due to their habit of regularly feeding on the forest floor, robins are subject to predation by stoats and feral cats, with nests often being predated by rats.

Silvereye

The first time we notice these tiny birds may be in our gardens, as they flit among branches or come to bird tables. Silvereyes are also known as white-eyes and waxeyes because of the white circle of feathers surrounding their eyes. As these mossy green-grey birds move so rapidly, it is impossible to see all their plumage colours.

Large numbers of silvereyes migrated to New Zealand from Australia in 1856. Their success is due to their ability to adapt to varieties of habitat and diet. Silvereyes are widely seen in forests, scrub, mangroves, orchards and gardens from sea level to high country and offshore islands but the birds are scarce in tussock land and grasslands.

Primarily insectivorous, they eat a wide range of insects, including caterpillars, spiders, flies, cicadas and katydids and, with their specially modified bristled tongue, sip nectar from a variety of flowering shrubs. The birds are also fruit eaters, taking fruit from native trees, such as kahikatea, rimu and shrubs, as well as blackberries and inkweed, so dispersing the seeds. Fruit in orchards and vineyards are sometimes damaged, as they favour sweet figs, cherries, apricots and grapes. But also called blightbirds, silvereyes readily eat garden pests like aphids, scale insects and greenfly, so compensate a little for spoilt fruit.

In early spring silvereyes build dainty cradle-like nests suspended within shrubs, hedges and outer branches of pine trees and bamboo. Made up of fine grasses, fibres, moss, lichen and thistledown, nests are tightly woven with spiders' web and lined with tiny leaves. They usually lay three eggs and the chicks are fed on insects, grubs and fruit.

After breeding, silvereyes form loose flocks, and especially in winter they move through gardens and parks searching for insects and fruit. The birds may suddenly arrive in a garden and where there is an abundance of food, the flock buzzes to and fro, as busy as, but faster than, bees. They call in excitable, high-pitched twitters but at other times whisper in soft, warbling trills among shrubbery. A pecking order exists within flocks and displays of wing fluttering and beak chattering indicate aggression.

Silvereyes are attracted to fat, fruit, sugar water and even breadcrumbs that can be made available to them on bird tables. In this way it is possible to observe their colours and behaviour closely.

149

Bellbird

Bellbirds occupy native forests, pine forests, scrublands, and some orchards and gardens, and are widespread in New Zealand, although absent from Northland. Their decline in Northland has been due to destruction of the forest, competition for tree flowers by possums and possibly avian disease. However, recently some birds have spread from offshore islands to a few northern predator-controlled locations.

With the name of bellbird, it would be assumed that they might call in a ripple of bell-like sounds and this was described well when Joseph Banks of Cook's *Endeavour* wrote in 1770. He was first woken at dawn by the sound of bellbirds: *'the most melodious wild music ... imitating small bells ... the most tuneable, silver sound imaginable ... '*. Bellbird songs can be heard throughout the year. While the birds are overall green, males have a purple gloss on their heads and ruby-bright eyes and females are duller with brown eyes.

The birds eat a variety of food and are valuable in the regeneration of native trees by assisting pollination in the course of nectar feeding, as well as spreading the seeds of the fruit they consume. They are one of the honey-eaters, having brush-tipped tongues that enable them to sip nectar and the honeydew found on the trunks of beech trees. Bellbirds also eat fruit and a wide range of invertebrates, such as spiders and grubs. It is known that males dominate at nectar sites, so females are compelled to feed more on insects. The birds are able to capture insects in mid-air, and also glean them from leaves. As well as flowers of native trees and shrubs, the nectar-bearing flowers of eucalypts and acacia trees in exotic forests have also proved attractive to bellbirds.

During courtship, males hover, flying slowly upwards and producing loud, whirring sounds with their wings. The birds maintain the same breeding territories year after year, and nesting times may vary in localities, but are usually between September and January. Bellbirds build their well-hidden nests in shrubs, crevices, behind vines or creepers or in the hollows of trees and often near a flowering tree. The nests are deep bowls that are loose constructions of grasses, twigs and fibre, lined with feathers and moss. The birds lay two to four eggs, and as they are very defensive around nest sites they may physically attack intruders. Chicks are fed on nectar, then insects and fruit. After the breeding season, birds tend to be solitary in their habits.

Tui

■ Widespread in forests, open country and urban areas.

■ Common.

■ Protected.

Length: 30 cm

Scientific Name:
Prosthemadera novaeseelandiae novaeseelandiae

Status:
Endemic

Tui, also once known as parson birds because of the two curled tufts of white feathers on their throats, are primarily forest birds. But they now occupy habitats throughout New Zealand, being familiar in urban gardens and parks. Tui are the largest of New Zealand's honeyeaters and they have adapted well in locations where flowering forest trees like puriri have been replaced by other nectar-producing plants.

The birds appear overall black, but their feathers combine colours of metallic dark turquoise and bronze contrasting with their white throat tufts and the lacy, filamentous white plumes lying against the backs of their necks.

Being honeyeaters, they search out nectar from forest tree flowers and shrubs, extracting it with long, brush-tipped tongues. Tui can be seen in summer taking nectar from pohutukawa and flax flowers along the coast and hanging upside down to sip from kowhai flowers. The birds also eat small forest berries and are valuable in dispersing the seeds of these plants and pollinating flowers, especially flax, mistletoe and puriri, as they carry pollen on their bills.

Insects, spiders, cicadas and wasps are nutritious supplementary food, as well as moths taken on the wing. Males tend to be dominant and aggressive when feeding, even denying females access to nectar, so, like bellbirds, females may consume more insect food.

Tui are known for their song and birds can often be heard calling well before dawn. Songs are clusters of notes sung rapidly, with melodic chimes and gongs, clicks, whistling bell notes and guttural croaks leading to a rich, fluid trill. Birds are usually solitary in habit, but form loose flocks and roosts during winter.

Their flight is strong and rapid, with their wings producing a whirring sound. They will soar above the forest canopy and then dive back into the forest.

The birds nest from September to January. Males are particularly defensive of their nest territory. Females build the bulky nests of sticks and dried grasses lined with feathers and soft grasses in tree forks, dense scrub or, where rats are a problem, high in kanuka trees. Tui lay two to four eggs and the chicks are then fed by both parents on nectar, berries and insects. Insects are important in providing protein for growing chicks.

Tui readily visit gardens where flowering trees and plants produce nectar and where sugar water is available in winter.

Yellowhammer

Widespread in open country, scrub and urban parks.

Common.

Length: 16 cm

Scientific Name: *Emberiza citrinella*

Status: Introduced

Yellowhammers are sparrow-sized birds introduced from Europe in the 1860s and are now widely distributed throughout New Zealand. They favour open country, scrub, sand dunes, rough grassland and saltmarshes and are also seen in the fringes of pine forests and subalpine bush. In winter large flocks congregate to feed on pastures and in shrubbery, often mingling with greenfinches and goldfinches, and clusters of the birds visit parks and gardens. Large flocks are particularly abundant on the margins of lupins and marram grass that have been planted near coastal pine plantations.

The sexes differ in plumage colour, with the males an overall bright yellow in colouring and the females a duller yellow and with more obvious brown striping on backs and wings. Females may also be confused with female cirl buntings as they are similar in size and colouring, with the noticeable difference being the chestnut rumps on yellowhammers. Cirl buntings are not so commonly seen, preferring the dry country of Marlborough and North Canterbury.

Yellowhammer pairs keep together during the summer, but flocks often gather to feed in winter. In the open country males are often seen singing from conspicuous posts or wires in high-pitched twitters and rambling notes. During flight, which is often undulating with a momentary closing of wings, the birds call with musical, metallic 'pink-pink' sounds.

They feed mainly on grass seeds, clover and weed seeds, also eating insects, spiders, grubs and worms that they find by poking around on the ground and among leaf litter. Yellowhammers sometimes feed on small, ripe fruit, especially blackberries. The winter flocks of birds wander to good food sources, such as spilt grain or stock food around buildings in farming districts. As the birds feed, they hop about searching through stubbly grasses and are not popular when they occasionally feed on newly sown seeds.

Early in the breeding season males chase females and parade with crests raised, tails spread and make curious bill-pointing gestures. The birds lay three or four eggs in nests made from dry grasses and moss, decorated with lichen and lined with horsehair, wool or feathers. They build their nests low in thick herbage on banks, and especially under brambles or hidden in gorse or clumps of dense grasses. Chicks are first fed on insects and later seeds. Like other ground-nesting birds, nests may be preyed on by magpies.

Chaffinch

■ Widespread in a variety of habitats, including forests.

■ Abundant.

Length: 15 cm

Scientific Name: *Fringilla coelebs*

Status: Introduced

These birds have become one of the most common finches in New Zealand, after being liberated here in the 1860s. At first they were slow to establish but are now abundant throughout the country in habitats extending from sea level to subalpine scrub. They do well where the land has been cultivated, such as farmlands, gardens and orchards, and are the only finches seen in native and exotic forests.

In winter chaffinches flock, sometimes mixing with other finches and sparrows as they feed, dropping lightly to the ground like the fluttering fall of brown leaves. They are easily identified with the males' rusty breast and powder-blue cap (lower photo) and the females' overall brown and grey-striped plumage (upper photo). Chaffinches are slimmer than sparrows and have distinctive white wingbars. Their short, conical bills are used to crush seeds.

Chaffinches feed on mixtures of seeds, invertebrates and small native tree fruits. They search out caterpillars and spiders, and other invertebrates such as flies, aphids and moths are sometimes caught on the wing, over streams and riverbeds. The birds favour seeds from cereal crops, brassicas, weeds and pine seeds that are pulled from newly opened cones. In winter large flocks of chaffinches congregate to feed on seeds in farmland, orchards and where grain is fed to animals and, in the South Island particularly, they gather to feed on fallen grain in cereal stubble fields. The birds sometimes cause damage to newly sown cereal crops, also eating new fruit buds, but do not seem to affect commercial orchards.

Chaffinches call in repetitive chirruping and short trills, punctuated with short 'zerp' sounds. They frequently call in metallic 'chwink-chwink's and in flight the birds may call in soft 'tsip' sounds. When males claim their nesting territories, they sing from high perches in loud, persistent short notes not only to attract mates but also to defend the sites from rivals.

Breeding pairs form in early spring and males display to females with a variety of little hops, moth flights and raised wings. In mid-September females build nests that are compact cups of dry grasses and moss, camouflaging them by pressing in lichen fragments and lining with feathers, wool and hair. Nests are usually set in forks of branches in manuka, shrubs, pine trees and willow. From late September to January they lay three to six eggs. The chicks are fed by both parents, and leave the nest at about 15 days.

Greenfinch

Greenfinches were introduced during the 1860s and are similar in size to sparrows. They are found throughout New Zealand in open country, cultivated land, waysides, gardens, parks and orchards, usually wherever there are protective trees nearby. The birds have benefited from the expansion of farming and especially the cultivation of cereal crops. They are also seen on rough land bordering pine plantations, where weeds may grow near cleared forest and where lupin and marram grass have been planted on sand dunes. In winter they flock near high-tide lines of harbours and in estuaries and are often seen in mangrove swamps.

The loud trilling of males is familiar in urban locations and their purring songs are especially evocative of the bird sounds of summer. The birds are known for a buzzing 'zzweee-zzweee' call, and when alarmed they can be heard calling in a canary-like 'tsooeet'. As they fly in an undulating, slow-motion 'butterfly' manner, similar to other finches, with rapid wing beats punctuated by a momentary closure, greenfinches sing in repetitive excitable twitterings.

Greenfinches feed on a variety of seeds and can easily pluck and crush hard seeds such as sunflower and maize in their strong conical bills. They can also often be seen feeding on blackberries and opening rosehips to extract the seeds as well as foraging on the ground for insects. The birds are sometimes considered to be pests as they take ripening grain and snip off fruit buds. They are sociable birds and in winter they form flocks, often together with yellowhammers and sparrows, to search for wild harvests of grass seeds, the seeds from thistleheads, and fallen grain in stubble fields. And particularly during winter, the flocks of birds often share communal roosts, in bamboo or thick foliage.

From mid-October to January birds pair off and form nesting territories. Greenfinches form bulky, fairly shallow nests of available grasses, moss and leaves, lining them with rootlets, fibres or feathers. The nests are built in tall hedges or bushes and branches of pines or manuka trees as well as in gorse. Chicks are fed on regurgitated seed pulp and during this process males twist their heads from side to side. Both parents feed the chicks.

Unlike goldfinches and chaffinches, greenfinches are known to visit garden bird tables with sparrows and silvereyes.

Goldfinch

■ Widespread, except in forests.

■ Abundant.

Length: 13 cm

Scientific Name: *Carduelis carduelis*

Status: Introduced

These small, brightly coloured finches are collectively called 'charms'. Since the 15th century in Britain a 'charm of goldfinches' has been the apt term for flocks of these fluttering, ornamental birds. Around 1860, homesick British settlers introduced goldfinches to New Zealand and they have adapted so well that they now outnumber those in their 'home' country. The features that help to distinguish the birds are their bright red facial masks and golden feathers in the green and black upperwings.

They prefer open country, roadsides, thickets, orchards and gardens, wherever wild seeded plants may grow, and especially thistleheads. The birds are primarily seedeaters and find habitats to suit them throughout New Zealand, except for the forests and wetter areas such as the West Coast, and they are not commonly seen above the bushline.

Goldfinches prefer to peck seeds from plants rather than gather fallen seeds. Favourite seeds are thistleheads and tall weeds, where the birds can be seen hanging upside down to extract seeds. They also feed on dried grass seeds of short pastures, and flocks of them sometimes move over the ground in a rolling or leapfrog manner, with the birds continually fluttering over the flock from rear to front. On cultivated land goldfinches find varieties of seeds, and like to nibble the tiny seeds on ripening strawberries, so damaging the fruit. Invertebrates are eaten to supplement their diet, more particularly during the breeding season, when chicks are fed with small insects to provide protein.

In spring the birds pair off, nesting in conifers, hedges, gorse, peach and apple trees as well as grapevines. In forks of narrow branches, they build nests that are delicate cups of fine twigs, dried grasses, lichen, moss and wool entwined with spiders' webs and lined with thistledown and downy feathers. They lay three to six eggs and the chicks leave the nest at 14 days.

During autumn and winter, flocks or charms of several hundred, sometimes even a thousand, goldfinches mingle with other finches on favoured feeding grounds. Apart from the seeds of wild weeds and thistles, the birds have been seen on sea banks of salicornia. Goldfinches draw attention with their fluttering, butterfly-like flight and the soft, twittering calls that are constant trickling sounds of 'tswitt-witt-witt'.

These birds thrive in New Zealand where there are still waysides of weeds and banks of gorse and thistle.

House sparrow

■ Widespread,
especially near
human
habitation.
Not found in
Fiordland.

■ Abundant.

Length: 14 cm

Scientific Name:
Passer domesticus

Status: Introduced

With such a name, it is natural to assume that these stout little birds would dwell in close proximity to humans. They are perky, bustling opportunists, well known for flitting in and around wherever food scraps might have been left. House sparrows were liberated in New Zealand in the 1860s and soon inhabited most localities apart from forests and mountain ranges. They prefer regions occupied by humans: gardens, parks, arable farmland and orchards, with the birds unlikely to be seen in forests or alpine country. In effect, they are dependent on the settlements and activities of humans.

After breeding, the 'hosts' or flocks of sparrows gather in winter, feeding and resting closely together in trees, shrubs and buildings where they can be heard in their roosts, calling in loud, jingling choruses. Male sparrows (upper photo) are distinctively coloured, with deep brown markings, black bibs and grey caps while females (lower photo) are more drably marked in light, streaked brown.

Flight is usually direct with continued flapping and no suggestion of gliding movements. They call noisily in repeated chirruping and brief chirps, sometimes with double notes that lead into ripples of chirps and short whistles. In summer along paths and edgings of road dust, sparrows take dust baths. They shake their feathers through the dust, as they would in water, and then ruffle them rapidly before flying off.

Sparrows are omnivorous feeders, moving together in flocks to find seeds, fruits and invertebrates. They forage on the ground and in their chunky bills crush seeds and eat beetles, caterpillars, flies and spiders, sometimes also hawking the insects. Insect food is sought particularly when feeding chicks. They cause considerable damage to ripening corn crops and eat flower and leaf buds, cherries and grapes, spoiling the new shoots of vegetables and fruit blossom. Sparrows are often seen in streets and gardens, taking crumbs and scraps and even entering cafés, factories and stables. They survive well on such a varied diet and show some aggression at bird tables, in attempts to exclude others.

Males court females by chirruping at nest territories and hopping and quivering around them, then from September to January they build their nests in trees, bushes, buildings or cliff crevices and nest boxes. These are bulky, untidy dome-shaped structures made of grasses, stems and twigs, lined with feathers, in which they lay three or four eggs.

Starling

■ Widespread throughout New Zealand to the fringes of forests.

■ Abundant.

Length: 21 cm

Scientific Name: *Sturnus vulgaris*

Status: Introduced

Introduced to New Zealand in 1862–63, starlings soon spread throughout the country and now the birds are abundant in open pastureland and urban localities. They are highly social birds, often moving and feeding within the safety of tight flocks.

Starlings are black with a glossy sheen of green and violet and the plumage becomes glitteringly starlit in winter when each feather is tipped with white (upper photo). Gradually feathers are worn and spots disappear (lower photo), so by the breeding season adult birds are entirely glossy black. They are distinguished from blackbirds by their long, pointed yellow bills and particular strutting walk.

Even though starlings are primarily insectivorous, they eat a variety of food. The birds find most insects by probing into short pasture, proving beneficial to farmers in digging out harmful grass grubs. They also take worms, snails, spiders and caterpillars, usually from the ground but also by hawking in the air. Birds sometimes forage on the shoreline, finding caterpillars among lupins and sandhoppers along the tideline. As well as eating fruit, especially kahikatea and vineyard grapes, starlings sip nectar from flax and pohutukawa flowers.

Nesting birds seek holes in trees on the fringes of forests or use crevices in cliffs and buildings and readily occupy garden nest boxes. Birds tend to revisit nest sites through the year to maintain ownership. As farmers have found the birds useful, some have erected nest boxes along fences. Their nests are loosely formed with dried grasses, leaves and pine needles, lined with moss.

From nearby perches, birds defend their nesting territories by singing in rambling songs that include warbles, whistles and clicks, while stiffly flapping their wings. They usually lay four or five eggs and both parents feed the chicks.

After breeding, starlings gather again in flocks, and especially during winter very large roosts of hundreds and thousands of birds assemble at the same sites each evening. Usually tall, leafy trees are chosen and Phoenix palms in urban districts are favoured roosts. The birds take time to settle and as more arrive and rapidly disappear inside the foliage, they are exceptionally vocal. The high-pitched jingling calls become a shrill, shattering vibration of sound, slowly quietening to become a 'murmuration of starlings', as the birds are collectively known. Not until night has settled do the birds become so quiet that it would not be known they were there.

Myna

Mynas were introduced to New Zealand in the 1870s from Asia, but did not thrive in the cooler South Island climate, so are now more common in the northern districts of the North Island. Mynas, also known as Indian mynas and common mynas, are adaptable birds, inhabiting open country where there are trees or scrub, but they favour localities of human habitation. They are particularly noticeable as they scuttle across roads or stride along stony roadsides.

They are intelligent but wary birds and are very bold and purposeful in manner, fearlessly strutting about in public places and adept at avoiding cars, as they feed on insects killed by traffic. The vivid yellow marking surrounding their eyes accentuates the mynas' solid bills and their assertive glares. The primary coverts are white, but this is only obvious in flight, when the white wing patches easily identify the birds.

Mynas commonly feed on the ground, eating a wide variety of invertebrates, fruit and food scraps. They can be seen on short pasture and among leaf litter finding insects and worms, as well as taking advantage of recently ploughed land where grubs, worms and caterpillars are exposed. Mynas visit farm outbuildings where animals are fed, snapping up leftovers, just as they do in public places where food scraps have been left. They take nectar from flax flowers and fallen fruit in orchards and will readily attack nests of starlings and other small birds, although not necessarily to eat the chicks.

During winter, mynas often feed in flocks of 5 to 20 birds and many join communal roosts of several hundred birds, gathering in thick shrubs or bamboo and frequently occupying these roosts throughout the year. At roost, they produce a noisy chattering while settling for the night and again at dawn. Their territorial calls are rapid sequences of raucous, squawking sounds, often to maintain contact between pair bonds.

Pairs of birds retain the same territory through successive years and nest from November to January. Nests are built in tree cavities, earth banks or buildings. As well, the birds may evict other chicks, especially starlings and even kingfishers, from their nests and then occupy the sites. Nests are composed of grasses, twigs and leaves with the addition sometimes of string, plastic or paper. They lay three or four eggs and chicks are then fed on worms, crickets, caterpillars and stick insects.

North Island kokako

- Found in forests north of Taranaki and in sanctuaries.
- Rare.
- Threatened species; protected.

Length: 38 cm

Scientific Name: *Callaeas cinerea wilsoni*

Status: Endemic

A description that seems to suit these secretive forest birds with their haunting calls is that the '… *origins of these birds are lost in the mists of time*' (R.B. Sibson). Kokako belong to the ancient family of wattlebirds related to saddlebacks and the extinct huia. They are a threatened species and survive in unmodified, mixed podocarp forests of the central North Island, the Ureweras and North Taranaki and in mixed kauri forests in Northland. The decline in their population is due to destruction of their habitat, competition for food and predation of nests by possums, stoats and rats.

The most notable feature of kokako is their song, heard usually at dawn and dusk. The songs are a series of long, melodic, organ-like chords and half notes, followed by flute-like calls, clucks and mews. Pairs sing duet clusters of double-note melodies. The birds are weak fliers but can make level flights of at least 50 metres. They use their long legs and strong claws to progress through the forest by springing from branch to branch rather like squirrels. Their rounded wings help them maintain balance as they work their way up branches and then glide down again, before moving to another tree.

The birds are mainly vegetarians and depend on old, undisturbed forests for varieties of food. In late summer they feed on the fruits and succulent foliage of podocarp and hardwood trees and on berries of shrubs and vines. Insects are eaten especially when feeding chicks and found by using their strong bills to probe into decaying wood, gleaning scale insects from under leaves and bouncing along the forest floor, poking into moss and ferns. Foliage and fruits are often held parrot-fashion with one foot, while they chew off morsels.

Paired birds are seen mutually preening throughout the year. They begin nesting in November, building large nests consisting of a base of sticks over-laid with ferns, lichen and moss and hidden among branches or built in dense, tangled supplejack and in passion vines that grow over old trees. Kokako lay two or three eggs and chicks are fed on small insects and fruit pulp. The chicks have lilac-coloured wattles that do not hang loose but lie against the throat and these develop to blue when the juveniles are mature.

Many kokako have been relocated and now successfully breed where extensive predator control is in place on offshore islands and mainland island sanctuaries.

Saddleback

- Found in offshore island sanctuaries.
- Rare.
- Protected.

Length: 25 cm

Scientific Name: *Philesturnus carunculatus*

Maori Name: Tieke

Status: Endemic

Saddlebacks belong to the family of wattlebirds that include kokako and the extinct huia, and they were common in forests throughout the country in the 19th century. Because they frequently feed on the ground, they were predated by introduced rats and cats and disappeared from mainland New Zealand. Populations survived only on Hen Island and on islands off Stewart Island. They have since been successfully transferred to several predator-free islands. The birds are especially conspicuous on Tiritiri Matangi, where their loud, lively staccato song is the predominant greeting of bird sound on arrival at the island.

The birds have wide, chestnut-coloured bands across the back and wings, from which they derived their name, and the males' droopy wattles are twice the size of the females' wattles. Immature birds (lower photo) have similarly small wattles. Birds are seen in pairs in established territories that they permanently defend. They are noisy but weak fliers, unable to sustain height, but are constantly active, rapidly leaping and bouncing across branches. The most commonly heard call is a rapid 'cheeet, te-te-te-te' and other loud short, sharp notes and melodious calls. The birds constantly chatter as they move through the forest and in the breeding season saddlebacks are heard making a 'cartwheel' call, which is reminiscent of the repetitive slow, squeaking turnings of a cartwheel.

Saddlebacks are noisy and vigorous as they search for food, and they are regularly followed by fantails snapping up disturbed insects. They forage for insects on the ground by scratching through leaf litter and then gradually move to the upper canopy. As they claw their way around tree branches, the birds use their strong, chisel-shaped bills to prise off loose bark to locate insects and dig into rotting wood. They also batter at the bark to loosen insects and grubs and use their bills to uncurl dead leaves, searching out hidden case moth larvae. A favourite saddleback food is the weta, and these larger insects are often held in one foot while the birds gradually pull them apart with their bills. The birds also eat spiders and fruit and sip nectar, especially from flax flowers.

They nest from October to January, laying two or three eggs in shallow cups built from twigs, bark fragments, stalks and leaves, lined with fine grasses. Saddlebacks make their nests in tree holes, cavities and rock clefts. Both parents feed the chicks and the families remain together for several months.

White-backed magpie

■ Widespread in open country, except Westland.

■ Common.

Length:
41 cm

Scientific Name:
Gymnorhina tibicen

Status:
Introduced

White-backed magpies are the more common of the two species of Australian magpies seen in New Zealand that were introduced from Australia in the 1860s to help control pasture insect pests. They are found in the open country of both main islands of New Zealand, inhabiting pastures and cultivated land, especially where there are nearby shelter-belts of pines and macrocarpa for roosting and nesting. They are common in cleared hill-country land.

The birds are conspicuous on open grassland with their distinctive black-and-white markings. The white markings in females and juveniles are flecked with black, giving a grey appearance that distinguishes them from the males. The magpies' calls are unmistakeable loud, melodious warbles. From high perches, especially at dawn and dusk, they like to call in an undulating flute-like chorusing, described in a poem by Denis Glover as '*quardle oodle ardle wardle doodle*'. Magpies also readily mimic the calls of other birds.

On pastureland and ploughed fields, the birds peck and probe with their bills for crickets, worms and snails, also taking flies, spiders and lizards, and they have proved helpful to farmers by eating grass grubs. But, as well, magpies eat seeds, foliage and grain and take eggs from the nests of skylarks, pipits and other ground-nesting birds. They have been observed feeding young chicks to their own chicks and magpies also take mice and scavenge for carrion. The birds are now considered pests, as they are very aggressive, pull up seedlings and not only drive away native birds but also attack sheep and dogs.

The birds can be fiercely territorial during the breeding season and will read-ily assault intruders. They nest early in the year, sometimes as early as June, and lay three or four eggs. Their nests are bulky structures composed of sticks, grasses and pine needles, lined with sheep's wool and fine grasses, and these are built high in tall manuka, pine, gum or macrocarpa trees, in the crowns of tree-ferns and in coastal pohutukawa. Both parents feed the chicks and they remain together as a family group for several weeks. In some instances white-backed magpies have interbred with black-backed magpies, so that pied forms exist with variations in the black plumage.

Magpies are known for their playfulness, especially when they are observed in captivity.

Bibliography

Armstrong, Edward, A., *Birds of the Grey Wind*. London: Oxford University Press, 1940.

Gill, Brian and Moon, Geoff, *New Zealand's Unique Birds*. Auckland: Reed Publishing, 1999.

Guthrie-Smith, H., *Birds of the Water, Wood and Waste*. Whitcombe & Tombs, 1927.

Hosking, Eric and Flegg, Dr Jim, *Eric Hosking's Owls*. London: Pelham, 1982.

Lockley, R.M. and Cusa, N.W., *New Zealand Endangered Species*. Auckland: Cassell, 1980.

Moon, Geoff, *New Zealand Birds In Focus*. Willoughby, NSW: Weldon, 1988.

Moon, Geoff, *New Zealand: Land of Birds*. Auckland: New Holland Publishers, 2001.

Moon, Geoff, *A Photographic Guide to Birds of New Zealand*. Auckland: New Holland Publishers, 2002.

Moon, Geoff, *The Reed Field Guide to New Zealand Birds*. Auckland: Reed Publishing, 2004.

Moon, Geoff and Lockley, Ronald, *New Zealand's Birds*. Auckland: Heinemann, 1982.

Robertson, Hugh and Heather, Barrie, *Field Guide to the Birds of New Zealand*. Auckland: Viking, 1996.

Sibson, R.B., *Birds at Risk*. Wellington: A.H. & A.W. Reed, 1982.

Soper, M.F., *Birds of New Zealand and Outlying Islands*. Christchurch: Whitcoulls, 1984.

Index